THE NEW
RULES
OF THE
ROAD

DAN
KAHN

THE **NEW**

RULES

OF THE

ROAD

HOW TO NAVIGATE THE
RAPIDLY CHANGING
MARKETING LANDSCAPE

Advantage | Books

Published by Advantage Books, Charleston, South Carolina.
An imprint of Advantage Media.

ADVANTAGE is a registered trademark, and the Advantage colophon is a trademark of Advantage Media Group, Inc.

Printed in the United States of America.

10 9 8 7 6 5 4 3 2 1

ISBN: 978-1-64225-691-8 (Hardcover)
ISBN: 978-1-64225-690-1 (eBook)

Library of Congress Control Number: 2024921304

Cover design by Analisa Smith.
Layout design by Matthew Morse.

This publication is designed to provide accurate and authoritative information in regard to the subject matter covered. It is sold with the understanding that the publisher is not engaged in rendering legal, accounting, or other professional services. If legal advice or other expert assistance is required, the services of a competent professional person should be sought.

Advantage Books is an imprint of Advantage Media Group. Advantage Media helps busy entrepreneurs, CEOs, and leaders write and publish a book to grow their business and become the authority in their field. Advantage authors comprise an exclusive community of industry professionals, idea-makers, and thought leaders. For more information go to **advantagemedia.com**.

To Sheridan—the wisest, kindest, and best person I know—
thank you for supporting me on this journey.

CONTENTS

ACKNOWLEDGMENTS

About sixteen years ago, I was working for a small but well-known PR firm on some pretty amazing accounts, making a good salary, and enjoying the newlywed life with my beautiful bride, Sheridan, who worked in the aerospace industry. We enrolled in an MBA program together, and within a few weeks, I figured a few things out: (1) she is a *much* better student than I am, and (2) I'm not great at sitting in a classroom and learning about business from books and lectures. I promptly dropped out of the program, and while she continued to work full time and earn her degree at night, I spent my now free evenings researching and learning about the massive changes about to hit the PR world, including a tidal wave of technology that was poised to crush the traditional corporate-owned media model and create a massive pivot to independent creators and platforms, allowing brands to communicate with consumers directly for the first time.

Those long nights of research eventually culminated in a business plan for a new type of agency. I brought that blueprint to the owner of the agency where I worked at the time, and while he was respectful of my position and my ideas, he didn't see the value of a major pivot and frankly told me to just keep doing my job. Once I make up my mind about something, however, it's pretty hard to get me to change course. My wife saw me growing ever more frustrated working under the "this is how we've always done it" leadership style and eventually encouraged me to leave and put my ideas into practice by starting my own agency. I worried about things like money and healthcare, and her response was "I can handle that for now; just try it. If it works, great. If not, you can always get another job." Those three simple sentences of support and encouragement were all I needed to go off on my own and start something new. And in all the years since, her love and support have allowed me to celebrate wins, recover from setbacks, and keep driving forward.

To Sheridan and our three beautiful children, Kennedy, Kaitlyn, and Hunter, I say thank you. Thank you for allowing me to chatter every night about cars and PR and new creator relationships and media outlets and all the stuff you realistically don't care all that much about because you know it's important to me. Thank you for keeping me grounded when I'm too full of myself and thank you for your love and support when a setback spins me out. This book wouldn't have happened without your support.

To my team at Kahn Media, thank you for teaching me far more than I've ever taught you about PR, marketing, leadership, and creativity. It wasn't until I reached middle age that I finally realized that the secret to wisdom is knowing you're not the smartest person in the room, so stop talking long enough to learn from those around you. And you fine folks have given me a master class in modern marketing—I hope to continue to learn from all of you for years to come.

For his wisdom, inspiration, and providing the spark that pushed me to do everything written about above, I'd like to thank David Meerman Scott for his pivotal book *The New Rules of Marketing & PR*, which first appeared as a free ungated e-book and then was published in print in 2007. Reading that book was such a seminal experience that it pushed my career path into an all-new direction and continues to inspire me today. I'd also like to thank Linda Pophal and the team at Forbes Books for their constant encouragement and help during this process. I literally could not have done this without you.

To Cory Burns, we've worked together across two companies for nearly half our lives—thank you for your loyalty, your hustle, and for being the "people person" part of our equation. We make a great team.

INTRODUCTION

The idea for this book came to me during the opening of a museum exhibit we were promoting. The exhibit focused on the Belle Époque era, a fascinating period of transition between the Enlightenment and World War I. This era saw Europe and the United States teetering between the old world of horse-drawn carriages and candlelight and the new age of industrial cities, factories, and automobiles. The transformation was as jarring as it was thrilling. Imagine cities like London, Paris, and New York enforcing "red flag" laws that required drivers of early motor cars to hire someone to walk in front of their vehicle with a red flag, warning horse riders of the approaching automobile. These laws, while meant to prevent accidents, ironically defeated the purpose of the car by slowing it down to a crawl. By the end of the Belle Époque, however, the red flag laws were gone, horses had mostly disappeared from city streets, and the urban landscape had become faster, louder, and more chaotic.

Was it better? Or just faster? Perhaps it was both. The agrarian age had given way to the industrial age. Today, we find ourselves in a similar period of transition, particularly in the realms of marketing, media, and public relations. At the start of my career, just a quarter of a century ago, most media were either TV or print (magazines and newspapers). Photography was done on film, and a marketer could do their job with nothing more than a phone and the contact info for a few publishers and magazine or newsroom editors. A marketing plan back then was like turning on a fire hose to fill your bucket.

Today, that fire hose doesn't even exist. Instead, it takes dozens, if not hundreds, of garden hoses set on trickle to fill that same bucket. Earned, owned, and paid media channels all need constant attention. Social channels need constant attention. Affiliate marketing programs require nonstop support. Influencer and creator marketing are effective but demand diligence. Paid media now encompass everything from traditional advertising to paid social, paid video on YouTube, streaming, over-the-top content, influencer shout-outs, and more. Order has given way to chaos, and PR is harder than ever because the traditional media business model has melted down. Magazines have mostly disappeared, and those that remain are either paper-thin gossip rags or subscriber-supported high-quality coffee table–style books. Most newsrooms have abandoned having large salaried staffs and instead get copy from freelancers paid not for context and quality but for click rates and eyeballs. Influencers are happy to work with brands, but are they media? Something else? Meanwhile, getting traditional outlets to cover a business, particularly a small business, is harder than ever, as local journalism has all but vanished.

But don't worry; all is not lost. Like all transitional periods in history, this one is rife with opportunity. Those who can figure out how to make current and future trends and technologies work in their favor will stake a claim in a new world that will allow them to dominate. Imagine being the first to buy Apple stock during its IPO or the first to secure URLs at the onset of Web 1.0—we have similar opportunities today.

This book is about navigating these turbulent times and coming out on top. We will explore how the landscape of PR and marketing has evolved, the challenges that come with it, and the strategies that will help you thrive. Drawing from my own experiences and the lessons learned from various campaigns and client interactions, we will delve into the intricacies of modern PR and marketing. We'll discuss the importance of agility, the power of storytelling, and the need for authenticity in an age where trust is more valuable than ever.

In the following chapters, we will journey through the complexities of today's PR and marketing world. We'll examine the critical role of data and analytics, the rise of influencer marketing, the shift toward direct-to-consumer (D2C) strategies, and the ever-growing importance of social media. We'll also look at how to manage crises effectively, maintain a strong brand reputation, and leverage new technologies to stay ahead of the curve.

This book is not just a guide; it's a road map for anyone looking to succeed in the dynamic and often unpredictable world of modern PR and marketing. Whether you're a seasoned professional or just starting out, the insights and strategies shared here will help you navigate the rough terrain and emerge victorious.

We're going to explore the opportunities that lie ahead, embrace the changes, and learn how to thrive in the ever-evolving landscape of PR and marketing. The road to success may be challenging, but with the right strategies and a forward-thinking mindset, we can not only navigate it but also lead the way.

THE TIMELESS PRINCIPLES OF PR

"The three main elements of public relations are practically as old as society: informing people, persuading people, or integrating people with people. Of course, the means and methods of accomplishing these ends have changed as society has changed."

Edward Bernays, often referred to as the "father of public relations," said that—in 1952! What's astounding is that these three main elements of public relations, or PR, are still valid today, despite the fact that at the time Bernays wrote them (fresh off PR stunts to promote smoking as a women's rights movement and bananas as a stand-in for democracy—more on that later), the radio was still considered fairly new tech. Despite the rampant advancement of communication and digital technologies, those who choose to dismiss these key fundamentals make a foolish mistake.

But—and this is an important but—the PR practice today is vastly different from how Bernays and his contemporaries practiced the art of connecting with, engaging, and influencing others. Today we have a mix of old and new communication channels and old and new approaches to how we leverage intermediaries (traditionally, media outlets and now more often influencers and other partners) to reach our audiences.

We have both more control and less leverage over how our messages reach the masses—and what happens once they do. To illustrate, let's take a look at two vastly different approaches taken by two twenty-first-century CEOs to promote their companies' electric vehicles—one traditional and one defying tried-and-true PR best practices or, in truth, ignoring PR best practices altogether.

EVERYTHING OLD IS NEW AGAIN

On one hand, we have Elon Musk, the maverick CEO of Tesla, who threw a massive party called the Cyber Rodeo at Tesla's Gigafactory in Texas in 2022. Musk strutted onto the stage wearing a cowboy hat and aviator sunglasses, captivating the audience as he unveiled the latest advancements in electric vehicles and self-driving technology. At the event he announced over-the-top updates for Tesla's autopilot feature, showcased his vision of the pickup truck of the future—the all–stainless steel Cyber Truck—and teased the Cyber Taxi, a fully autonomous two-seater vehicle. The event was live streamed on Tesla's own channels, bypassing traditional media outlets entirely.

In fact, Musk had previously fired all his PR staff and invited no PR people or media representatives to the party. And yet, the coverage and buzz were exceptional and positively charged, gaining traction in outlets like TechCrunch, the Verge, CNBC, the *Wall Street Journal*, Fox Business, and a host of others, as well as generating commentary like this brand-supportive coverage by the *Wall Street Journal*:[1]

"The party kicked off Thursday afternoon inside Tesla's factory, where electronic music blared and displays introduced visitors to Tesla's manufacturing process. Employees, contractors and superfans such as Jen Ragen walked the vast factory floor on self-guided tours of tooling and partially assembled Model Ys. Ms. Ragen, 38, said she bought her first Tesla, a Model S luxury sedan, in 2014. 'Once you drive these vehicles, you can't stop obsessing,' said Ms. Ragen, who drove 1,600-plus miles from Philadelphia in her Model Y to be part of the factory's public debut."

Contrast this with coverage that was sought and received by Ford and its CEO, Jim Farley, a marketing expert who rose to fame, first at Toyota, where he created the Scion brand to target Gen X American consumers, moving up the ranks until jumping to Ford, first in a marketing role and eventually as CEO. He planned and personally

---

1   Rebecca Elliott, "Tesla to Host 'Homecoming Cyber Rodeo' in Texas,'" the *Wall Street Journal*, October 29, 2023, https://www.wsj.com/articles/tesla-to-host-homecoming-cyber-rodeo-in-texas-11649323802.

led a road trip with the electric F-150 Lightning during the summer of 2023 from San Francisco to San Diego.

JIM FARLEY: TRADITIONAL PR MEETS REALITY

Farley's trip was a well-choreographed publicity stunt and an attempt to showcase the truck's capabilities and promote electrification by visiting dealers and customers along the route. He documented the trip on social media, hoping to create a curated story for the media to cover. But Farley's trip didn't go as planned. He faced challenges with third-party charging stations, resulting in long waiting times and frustrated drivers, including Farley himself. The experience—specifically designed for all to see—highlighted the real-world issues with EV-charging infrastructure and generated negative publicity for Ford. Like this from Yahoo Finance:

"Owning an electric vehicle (EV) isn't the stuff road trip dreams are made of, as Ford's CEO Jim Farley realized recently when he took the company's electric F-150 Lightning on a road trip from Silicon Valley to Las Vegas."[2]

The situation got worse. Coinciding with Farley's trip, a Ford customer's nightmare journey in a Ford EV that broke went viral on social media. The customer experienced multiple issues with their electric vehicle, ultimately needing to rent a car to get home. They got stuck so many times that it bricked the car, and they finally had to have it towed to a dealership to get fixed. As this issue unfolded and the customer documented it on social media—and because it was happening at the exact same time as the CEO's similar road trip—the

---

2   "Charging Is Pretty Challenging," Says Ford's CEO," *Yahoo Finance*, June 14, 2024, https://finance.yahoo.com/news/charging-pretty-challenging-fords-ceo-110000710. html.

story got picked up by the national media and drove home some pretty tough points for the Dearborn-based automaker.

Clearly not the narratives that Ford was looking for in support of its product. But, to his credit, Farley transparently acknowledged the issues he faced and didn't step back from the criticism. Yet damage to the brand—and the future of EVs—was certainly done.

MUSK'S PR SUCCESSES DEFY TRADITION

Despite Musk's polarizing qualities and questionable social antics, his example is illustrative of today's new PR landscape precisely because Musk has eschewed what has long been believed to be the gold standard in PR practices. Musk's contrary approach works.

The Cyber Rodeo isn't the only example. When Musk launched his personal Tesla Roadster into space on a SpaceX Falcon Heavy rocket, manned by a dummy he dubbed "Starman," the media reaction was equally significant. The event captured the imagination of the public and generated widespread media coverage and social media commentary. The image of a spacesuit-clad mannequin in the driver's seat of the Roadster as it soared through space provided a powerful visual that was simply impossible to ignore. As *Inc.* reported: "The Space X Heavy Falcon [sic] launch was a smashing success in many ways. But to me, it was the cargo that Elon Musk sent aboard the rocket that made the biggest impact. It was Marketing genius."[3] This unconventional PR stunt showcased Musk's ability to create buzz and excitement around his companies and their visions for the future, while also demonstrating the power of direct-to-consumer communication in the digital age.

---

3   Gary Golden, "Elon Musk Launching His Personal Tesla Roadster into Space Is Pure Marketing Genius. Here's Why," *Inc.*, June 14, 2024, https://www.inc.com/gary-golden/elon-musk-launching-his-personal-tesla-roadster-into-space-is-pure-marketing-genius-heres-why.html.

THE EVOLUTION OF PR: MY JOURNEY

I'm fortunate that my career in PR has spanned the evolution of PR from wooing—and often wining, dining, and regaling—media gatekeepers to taking control of the messaging and taking it directly to consumers through the many and varied digital communication channels that now exist. From work as both a journalist and a PR practitioner in agency environments to launching my own firm, Kahn Media, a modern PR firm working at the cutting edge of both the broad market and specialist markets, I've truly seen it all. Today, as the agency for companies like Rolex, Maserati, Peninsula Hotels, and Lotus, among many others, we use innovative strategies to form direct relationships with consumers, blending the old and new ways of PR to achieve maximum return on investment for our clients.

In the old world of PR, there were three primary pathways to exposure for brands and their products and service: earned, owned, and paid. Earned media is the coverage brands receive through their PR efforts like news stories in print or broadcast media. Owned media is the brand's own content. Paid media is advertising.

But the traditional silos of earned, owned, and paid media have started to erode, and today there is more crossover and integration between these categories. Companies, regardless of their size, now have the ability—and the opportunity—to communicate directly with audiences of all kinds with few if any barriers. They no longer need to rely on the traditional multistep distribution model of media and PR. Instead, they can leverage their own media channels and their own content—as Musk and others have done and will increasingly continue to do—to tell their own stories.

NAVIGATING COMPLEX PR LANDSCAPES

New technology and changing consumer habits have accelerated the shift to—and the influence of—a direct-to-consumer media market. This shift has dramatically changed the channels where PR is practiced and has amplified the efficacy of PR while making it more targeted and measurable than traditional advertising in many cases.

There have never been fewer barriers to entry for brands that want to engage audiences. There have never been more tools to measure results or data points to track. But these new opportunities present many additional complexities. Agencies like Kahn Media are uniquely positioned to master these kinds of complexities.

Having looked at the broad trend of how public relations and marketing have changed drastically, we can now dive into the history of PR and explain how the early days of print, the advent of cable news in the 1990s, and the rise of modern spectacle-and-outrage culture have set the stage for clever operators to prosper in the modern media era.

By understanding where we've come from, we can better navigate where we're going. This book is your guide to thriving in this new era of PR and marketing. Let's explore together how to leverage these changes to build stronger, more resilient brands that can not only survive but thrive in the ever-evolving landscape of modern communication.

CHAPTER 1

THE ROAD THAT LED HERE

(THE HISTORY OF PR AND MARKETING)

P ublic relations—or PR—has always existed in some form, but it truly took flight in the era of mass media and has continued to evolve to the digital times we live in today. Its practice has changed significantly, as we'll see.

THE BANANA MAN: SAMUEL ZEMURRAY'S PR PROWESS

Samuel Zemurray, known as the "banana man,"[4] was a self-made mogul who went from being a penniless roadside banana peddler to becoming a kingmaker and capitalist revolutionary. A Russian

---

4   Rich Cohen, *The Fish That Ate the Whale: The Life and Times of America's Banana King* (Farrar, Straus and Giroux, 2012).

immigrant who arrived in the United States in the early 1890s, Zemurray landed on the docks of New Orleans. He found a job unloading bananas—referred to as "ripes"—from boats. Like most people at the time, Zemurray had never seen a banana before, but as he searched for a way to make a living, he saw an opportunity in the banana business.

One key observation was that even a single brown spot on a bunch of bananas would lead to the entire bunch being thrown away. Sensing an opportunity, he made a deal with the dock workers: he would take all the bananas they were going to toss, even if they were nearly rotten. Then he figured out a distribution mechanism. He called all the grocers serving the lower- and middle-class people living along a rail spur line leaving the port in New Orleans. He would hustle the bananas onto a train car and bribe the train conductor to let him have just one carload. At every stop along the railroad, grocers would be waiting, and he'd unload as much as they wanted, receiving cash in return.

Zemurray's success led him to eventually buy his own boat, then his own ship, and finally land in Central America to grow bananas. He established the largest privately owned marine fleet in the Western Hemisphere. In fact, during the Spanish-American War, it was his boats the government used to go to war, as the US Navy was actually quite small at the time. His rise in the industry ultimately put him at the top of it. After founding the Cuyamel Fruit Company, which was later bought out by United Fruit, Zemurray took over the entire organization—one that still exists today, under a different name: Chiquita Banana.

USING PR AND PROPAGANDA TO SELL BANANAS

One of Zemurray's initial challenges was introducing the banana to Americans and convincing them it was good for them. Enter Edward Bernays. Bernays, the nephew of Sigmund Freud, was well versed in human psychology and its implications for influence. He wrote several books, including *Crystallizing Public Opinion* and *Propaganda,* which laid the groundwork for modern public relations.

Bernays knew he needed a clever idea to make bananas popular. He hired doctors to write articles claiming that bananas were a superfood capable of curing various ailments. In Hollywood and New York, he supplied bananas to hotels and restaurants known to serve celebrities and famous leaders and then hired photographers to take pictures of the high-profile people eating them. He even created a fake holiday called "National Banana Day" to promote the fruit. But Bernays's most successful idea was to create a "news service" called the Middle America Information Bureau, which supplied articles and news feeds to journalists around the country, mostly stories seeded with positive spin on bananas, the fruit trade, and even the central American countries where the yellow fruits were grown. The stunt was a huge success, and the media coverage helped make bananas a popular fruit in America.

FROM SELLING BANANAS TO OVERTHROWING GOVERNMENTS

Bernays and Zemurray did far more than just sell bananas; their collaboration wasn't always ethical. Bernays lobbied hard for the overthrow of Guatemala's reformist president Jacobo Arbenz, who dared to take on United Fruit in the early 1950s based on their labor and land-use practices. Bernays helped mastermind the war for Zemurray and

United Fruit, drawing on every PR tactic and strategy he had refined since giving birth to the profession forty years earlier.

Their relationship illustrates the dual nature of PR—it can raise awareness and inform, or it can mislead and manipulate. While many of Bernays's actions fall into the latter category, he is still remembered as the father of modern PR. The experiences that Zemurray and Bernays had in creating a "banana empire" through early applications of PR principles marked the beginning of understanding and leveraging media for shaping and shifting public sentiment.

THE EVOLUTION OF "THE MEDIA"

The early notion of PR and marketing was focused largely on manipulating people and planting ideas, much like Zemurray and Bernays did. Monikers like "snake oil salesmen" and "hucksters" were used to refer to hawkers and carnival barkers prevalent in the late nineteenth and early twentieth centuries peddling fraudulent or dubious products like patent medicines.

Before media outlets as we know them today began to emerge in the 1920s with the introduction of local and national broadcast (radio) alongside print media, information had to be shared person to person—reach was limited. Newspapers, followed by radio and then television, provided outlets that allowed those who wanted to share information to do so far more simply and with far more impact.

Bernays believed in the "hypodermic model" of media, also known as the "magic bullet theory." This model suggests that the media can precisely influence an audience by injecting messages directly into their minds. The message is the magic bullet—or hypodermic needle—that can be implanted into individuals' minds to shape their beliefs.

This model was more prevalent during a time when there were limited sources of information and fewer competing messages. It was also a time when there was a high level of trust in the media. People were much less critical of the content they consumed. Back in the days of Bernays, the media landscape consisted of tiers starting at the national level down to local media outlets, initially through newspapers. Any message injected into this media funnel—starting at the national level and trickling down into local markets—could potentially influence public opinions.

Up until the early 1900s, the media landscape was significantly different from what we know today. Life was very local, confined to relatively small geographic bounds. Most small towns relied on newspapers as their primary source of information. Most of these newspapers were privately owned and operated, often by family businesses. Even in larger cities, newspapers at the time were owned by single families, like the Chandlers, who owned the *Los Angeles Times*, or the Sulzbergers, who owned the *New York Times*.

In the early twentieth century, this began to change. Newspapers started to play a more dominant role as market intermediaries, connecting sellers—advertisers—and buyers in local areas. This led to a change in content and design as newspapers attempted to appeal to a broader audience that included women, the working class, and immigrant readers. The decentralization of media ownership was further disrupted by the rise of broadcast media, leading to the creation of national networks that could reach a wider audience.

Initially, radio was the game changer but still very localized. Stations weren't able to push signals out very far, and they were mostly independently owned and operated. Then things really started to get interesting in PR.

THE RISE OF TELEVISION AND NATIONAL MEDIA NETWORKS

During the period between World War I and World War II, television emerged, introducing ABC, NBC, CBS, and then national radio stations with repeaters that could push the same signal to cities all over the country. Some of the bigger papers like the *New York Times* grew to the point where they were being read outside their local geography.

This is when PR became a more powerful tool. Suddenly, with the right strategy and the right people applying that strategy, you could reach millions of people—all over the country, even all over the world.

DEREGULATION AND THE CONSOLIDATION OF MEDIA MARKETS

In the 1990s, the US government relaxed regulations in the media industry, allowing for increased competition and consolidation. The 1996 Telecommunications Act, signed by President Clinton, removed conflict-of-interest restrictions on major-media ownership, allowing companies from different industries to own media outlets. The result: national media ownership dropped from sixty-two entities in 1996 to six near-monopolies that controlled 90 percent of national media outlets.[5]

This deregulation brought about a seismic shift that has reshaped how we consume and disseminate information. It's a double-edged sword, presenting both opportunities and challenges for PR professionals, marketers, and society at large.

---

5   "Businesses Press Congress to Ease Immigration Rules amid Labor Shortage," *AP News,* June 14, 2024, https://apnews.com/article/business-immigration-deregulation-f2021dc7425a4001b1f910a3bb075b87.

THE MODERN MEDIA LANDSCAPE

Imagine a vast river, once fed by numerous tributaries, now merging into one colossal body of water. This is the media landscape today. The sheer volume of content sources means there's a niche for everyone, no matter how specific or obscure. Want to immerse yourself in a singular viewpoint? There's a site, subsite, newsfeed, content creator, YouTube channel, and Twitter feed waiting for you. This proliferation has given rise to echo chambers, where individuals can easily cocoon themselves, only hearing and validating their own perspectives without external voices.

However, while the surface appears diverse, the undercurrent tells a different story. At the global level, we've circled back to a time where only a handful of sources dominate the information flow. This is largely due to corporate ownership. Super groups, born out of deregulation, now own a vast array of local and regional TV stations, affiliates, national networks, and even newspapers. The result? A single story can be replicated across hundreds of outlets, each parroting the same script. It's a PR person's dream, but it raises questions about the diversity and authenticity of the content we consume.

THE RISE OF CABLE NEWS AND ITS IMPACT ON PR

The impact of this can be seen through the rise of cable news. Channels like CNN, Fox News, and MSNBC emerged and grew, each adopting distinct formats and readily discernible political leanings. The rise of cable news in the 1990s marked a significant turning point for journalism and PR. Before, news was delivered through scheduled broadcasts, and there was a clear distinction between news and advertising. Cable news, with its twenty-four-hour news cycle, blurred the lines and dissolved the traditional "firewall" between news and content.

With the need to generate content around the clock, news outlets couldn't just rely on traditional news stories. They soon learned to use outrage and alarm to attract viewers. Sensationalism, controversy, and emotionally charged stories became the norm. For PR professionals, this meant that stories with a sensational or controversial angle had a higher chance of gaining traction.

The news cycle has also become much shorter. With continuous news, PR professionals have to be always "on," ready to manage their client's image, respond to crises, or capitalize on opportunities quickly. Events that once dominated headlines for months now barely last a day.

THE ESSENCE OF PR AND THOUGHT LEADERSHIP

PR is all about managing perceptions by creating and sharing messages designed to influence how an audience—whether customers, prospects, employees, or the general public—thinks about your business and its products and services. But it goes beyond simply sharing information. It's about telling a compelling story that resonates with your audience while driving your strategic goals and achieving desired outcomes. The goal isn't just to "spin" a message—it's to create and sustain relationships. After all, "relations" is right there in the term itself.

Thought leadership is closely connected to PR but is specifically focused on establishing your company or members of your company as experts at the forefront of your industry. Your thought leaders are the people from your organization speaking at conferences, writing articles or white papers, or engaging in conversations on social media. They're trusted resources and stand out in meaningful ways from others in the same space. The goal isn't to be like everyone else—it's to be different in a compelling way.

EARNED, OWNED, AND PAID MEDIA

Businesses today wanting to get their messages in front of key audiences have three opportunities: owned, earned, and paid media. These options have always existed—they've just changed significantly over the years.

Owned media are channels that business owners have complete control over. Pre-internet, this might include things like direct sales or events. Today, most businesses have websites and social media channels that allow them to get their messages out to far more people than ever before.

Earned media is what has historically been referred to as public relations or media relations. It's coverage that is "earned" by interesting gatekeepers in what you have to say, so they agree to share those messages with their audiences. Big media outlets—like network and cable TV, newspapers, and radio to some degree—still play a role here, as do influencers. Earned media exposure is generally considered more credible since these messages aren't directly controlled by the brand.

Paid media, as it sounds, includes traditional advertising, sponsored content, and paid social media posts.

One of the biggest shifts here is in brands' ability to communicate directly with their audiences, something that was very difficult to do in the past and could only be done on a relatively small scale. Today, though, rapid shifts in their ability to connect with audiences directly through digital channels, and the explosion of opportunities for earned and paid media, have changed the PR communication landscape.

NEWSJACKING

David Meerman Scott coined the term newsjacking in his book *Newsjacking*. The book's subtitle explains the concept: *How to Inject Your Ideas into a Breaking News Story and Generate Tons of Media Coverage.*[6]

The original connotation of the term suggested there had to be something bad happening. At my agency, we've taken a different approach and been very successful with it. We don't think newsjacking is just about taking a crisis and spinning it. It's about saying, "Okay, knowing that the same basic story is being reported across the mainstream media, we can go in and say, 'Here's another piece of that story that we have to share.'"

That's exactly what we did when we were working with a very popular automotive lifestyle event that occurs in Monterey, California, every August—The Quail, A Motorsport Gathering. While the broader news narrative at the time hinted at a softening economy and impending recession, we found a different story to tell. Every August, Monterey becomes a mecca for vintage car enthusiasts. What began as a series of events centered around the vintage car collecting world, like the Pebble Beach Concours d'Elegance and the Rolex Monterey Motorsports Reunion, has evolved into a grand spectacle known as Monterey Car Week. Over the years, this event has grown in size and stature, attracting not just vintage car aficionados but also major car companies showcasing their latest models.

Of course, the landscape shifted dramatically during the COVID-19 pandemic. The auto show circuit, a staple in the car world, was severely impacted. In fact, the crown jewel of these shows, the Geneva Auto Salon, never recovered from the pandemic's blow.

---

6   David Meerman Scott, *Newsjacking: How to Inject Your Ideas into a Breaking News Story and Generate Tons of Media Coverage* (Wiley, 2011).

This left a void, and Monterey Car Week, with its unique blend of vintage charm and modern allure, was poised to fill it.

Suddenly, our motorsport gathering transformed from a quaint garden party car show into a global stage for new-car debuts. In a single day, we witnessed seventeen back-to-back press conferences in just six hours. From luxury brands like Porsche, Bentley, and Rolls-Royce to innovative newcomers like Kia showcasing their latest EVs, Monterey was buzzing. But what really captured our attention were the groundbreaking innovations on display. A company 3D-printed an entire car chassis using metal additive printing. Another, Koenigsegg, introduced a revolutionary electric motor that promised to redefine the EV landscape. This wasn't just a car show; it was a convergence of the world's brightest automotive minds and innovations.

Recognizing the potential, we pitched a unique angle to the mainstream business press. Here were individuals, from all corners of the globe, investing in seven- and eight-figure hypercars, placing deposits on futuristic tech—even flying cars. At a time when the news cycle was focused on a declining economy and impending recession, our message was clear and compelling: those with means were betting big on the future, undeterred by economic speculations. We placed four hundred stories on that event. It was all over the place—in outlets ranging from Bloomberg to Fox to Yahoo News, and all of the tech sites.

This is the essence of newsjacking. It's not just about spinning a crisis or jumping on a trending topic. It's about identifying underlying narratives, offering fresh perspectives, and enriching the broader story. In the ever-evolving world of PR, this approach not only captures attention but also shapes the discourse. To be successful in crafting these narratives, PR pros must be voracious consumers of content—reading multiple news outlets daily, understanding various viewpoints, and having a nuanced grasp of the media cycle. Only by staying informed can they identify opportunities to insert their narratives effectively.

DIRECT-TO-CONSUMER MARKETING

Direct-to-consumer (D2C) marketing is one way brands bypass gatekeepers and take control of their messaging. While D2C marketing is primarily a sales strategy, PR plays an important role and is deeply intertwined. PR is an ideal way for many organizations to engage with their customers to build brand narratives and trust.

The COVID-19 lockdowns were a catalyst in driving more people online. During the pandemic, even the most traditional shoppers found themselves navigating the online marketplace, integrating themselves into the digital marketing ecosystem. But the shift was already taking place even before the pandemic.

For decades, brands were tethered to a multistep distribution process where their products had to pass through multiple hands before reaching consumers. Giants like Amazon and Walmart entered the scene, but we were still a step away from truly connecting directly with our audience. Then came D2C. While the internet certainly moved us in this direction, the real revolution was fueled by brands like Shopify.

For example, when I started my agency, it cost a minimum of $100,000 to build a website. It was a huge amount of work. Today, building a website is pretty much a plug-and-play undertaking. I've built a couple for myself and one for my thirteen-year-old daughter, who has a pie business. We built an entire e-commerce site for her in about an hour using a template. It includes back-end capabilities like inventory control, the ability for people to buy pies online, and a direct connection with her bank so the money hits her account immediately. In the past, you'd need a bunch of web developers sitting in a dark room banging out code for weeks to make this happen. That's a real shift.

D2C is a game changer, not only because of better margins when you sell directly but also because of the connections you can make with your customers. Through D2C, we can engage with our consumers directly, hear their feedback, and tailor our offerings in real time. From a PR perspective, those insights are gold! We can observe our consumers, understand their behavior, and refine our strategies. Remember, in today's digital age, data is king. With D2C, we're not just generating sales; we're gathering invaluable first-party data. This allows us to understand our audience better and craft messages that resonate.

A SEA CHANGE IN PR

The evolution of the PR world and integrated marketing communications is truly fascinating. Just a decade ago, web PR was the underdog, while print media dominated the industry. In those days, PR agencies focused on obtaining print clips, primarily in magazines, as frequently as possible. The more clips, the better the perceived performance.

I recall my time at a PR agency where the owner assessed account teams based on "PR by the pound." At the end of each month, we would print out all our magazine hits, compile them into a binder with an executive briefing on top, and prepare them to be sent to the client. The agency owner would judge the binder's worth by the sound it made when dropped on his desk. A loud thud indicated a successful month, while a soft thud meant trouble.

However, the real challenge back then was measuring the true value of those pounds of print. One story in a single media outlet could have been a game changer, but there was no way to know.

Neither the agency owner nor the client could accurately measure public opinion, aside from correlating sales with media placements.

Proving the ROI of a PR campaign was like trying to catch smoke with your bare hands. But with the advent of modern tools, we now have real-time feedback and tracking capabilities. PR and integrated marketing practitioners can utilize tools like Looker Studio, Semrush, Qualtrics, HubSpot, ActiveVoice, and a multitude of others to evaluate campaign effectiveness. For the first time in history, the link between PR efforts and profit is demonstrable.

The instantaneous nature of PR in the digital realm is a game changer in our fast-paced world. Today, anyone with a voice and a vision can directly connect with their audience, creating genuine relationships. The game has changed. The competition for ad dollars remains, but the players have consolidated. The question we must grapple with is *In this new era, how do we maintain the integrity, diversity, and ingenuity that once defined the media industry?*

This new era of PR can be intimidating, especially for business owners with little background or interest in the field. We're in a Wild West moment, with digital technology, artificial intelligence, generative AI, and a decentralized media market dominated by freelancers and influencers. But this moment also presents immense opportunities. With a clear road map, understanding of core principles, and knowledge of where the industry is heading, you can stay ahead of your competitors and effectively communicate your message directly to your audience. This requires ensuring your organization is in an ideal condition to take advantage of these opportunities in ways that will be consistent and brand supporting across all communication channels.

It starts with an intimate and accurate understanding of your company, who you are, what you have to offer, and who you'll offer it to.

TAKEAWAYS

➔ How well have you adapted your PR strategies to the digital age? To what extent have tools like Google Analytics, social media platforms, and generative AI (GenAI) impacted how you connect with key audiences?

➔ Assess your ability to measure the return on investment (ROI) for your PR campaigns. How are you leveraging available tools to track and analyze the impact of your communications? How could you do a better job with this?

➔ To what extent have your PR campaigns influenced the opinions or behaviors of your target audiences?

➔ Consider the ethical implications of your PR efforts—are your campaigns designed to mislead or manipulate, or to inform and build genuine relationships?

CHAPTER 2

KNOW YOUR VEHICLE

On a dusty road in the middle of nowhere, a helicopter swoops in, and a man rappels down with a bag of coffee, landing through the sunroof of a moving vehicle. Meanwhile, another guy drives alongside them with a machine gun mounted on the back of an armored personnel carrier. Sound like a familiar action movie? Think again. This over-the-top, adrenaline-pumping scene is actually from a marketing video for Black Rifle Coffee Company, a firm that has mastered the art of knowing both their vehicle and target audience, bringing the two together in a compelling way.

QUALITY PRODUCT + TARGETED MESSAGING = ALIGNMENT

Black Rifle Coffee Company was founded by Matt Best and Evan Hafer—two veterans with a love for top-notch coffee. They wanted to build a brand that would hit home for folks in the service, first responders, and conservatives. They nailed it by truly understanding their product and who they wanted to reach. They get it.

While on active duty in the Middle East, Evan, a self-proclaimed coffee snob, struggled to find a good cup of coffee. He started having beans sent to him from the States, grinding and brewing them himself, and soon became the go-to coffee guy in his group. Recognizing the opportunity to create a high-quality product with a brand that aligned more closely with their target audience, Matt and Evan built Black Rifle Coffee Company on the foundation of a great product and a strong message.

They knew that if the coffee wasn't good, people wouldn't buy it, no matter how appealing the branding was. But the taste wasn't all that mattered. They built a brand that aligned with their target audience's values and beliefs, and they did it with a bold marketing approach that resonated with their customers.

Black Rifle Coffee Company got it—they didn't have to be everyone's cup of tea, or coffee in this case. They just had to win over the crowd they were aiming for, and that's exactly what they did. They started with their owned media, creating content that was bold, edgy, and sometimes over the top. Their marketing materials, like merchandise featuring the Gadsden flag (a historical American flag with a timber rattler over a yellow background with the words "Don't Tread on Me") with the slogan "Coffee or Die," were in line with their brand identity and appealed to their target audience of people in the service, first responders, and those with conservative values.

The company understood that they didn't need to please everyone but that they could be successful if they pleased those they identified as their target customers. They also ventured into owned media, like podcasts, and created attention-grabbing videos that went viral on social media, driving traffic and attention to their brand. Through their own media, they leaned into their message, incorporating a community social-good aspect by allowing customers to donate bags of coffee to members of the service and first responders. They also donated heavily to foundations supporting veterans with PTSD and other issues and were aggressive about hiring veterans for their leadership team and giving preference to veterans when opening franchise stores. Their marketing efforts were unapologetically bold.

By offering a strong and unique brand voice that was a major counterpoint to the traditional big chain coffee companies that try to be all things to all people, BRCC created more than a coffee company; they built a brand ethos people *wanted* to identify with. Customers buy Black Rifle Coffee Company merch and wear it proudly because it identifies them as part of a tribe. They listen to the podcasts, slap decals on their trucks, and support creators and influencers who are sponsored by the company.

The company's marketing approach is authentic and demonstrates a solid understanding of who they are and what they stand for. By staying true to their core values and target audience, they were able to create a cohesive and effective marketing strategy that resonated with their customers and set them apart from the competition.

BEYOND MESSAGING—YOU MUST HAVE A GREAT, DIFFERENTIATED PRODUCT

Now, let's flip the script and talk about Liquid Death. Picture this: a canned water brand sporting a wild death metal–style logo with a skull that's screaming its head off, all under the banner "Murder Your Thirst." Liquid Death targets a younger audience with unconventional and attention-grabbing marketing tactics, including outrageous and funny internet content. Their edgy tactics, like limited edition merchandise drops and collaborations, have garnered attention and helped them stand out in a crowded market.

One of the most notable marketing stunts Liquid Death pulled off was a collaboration with Travis Barker from Blink-182. They created a limited-edition enema kit featuring their sparkling water, playing off the band's popular album *Enema of the State*. Despite the bizarre nature of the product and a warning not to actually use it, people bought the enema kits, generating significant attention for the brand.

Their social media efforts are equally edgy and bizarre. For example, they created a video that appeared to show a person's daily water-drinking experience from the perspective of someone with a GoPro inside their mouth.

But, despite their unique marketing approach and brand awareness—or maybe because of it—Liquid Death has not yet reached financial solvency, as they spend a significant amount on brand and marketing stunts without building their company on a financially viable foundation. Think about it—a mostly naked Travis Barker lying on a rug and talking about literally taking their product and putting it where the sun doesn't shine. That's a pretty weird, and pretty unappetizing, message for a company trying to sell drinkable water.

So, what's the lesson to be learned from these two companies that, on the surface, seem to be taking a similar marketing communications approach? It's not just about marketing and marketing messages. It's also about product (and more things we'll talk about later).

Black Rifle Coffee Company has a great product and on-point, audience-specific messaging. Liquid Death sells water. It's a commodity with little uniqueness.

As we dive into this chapter, let the story of Black Rifle Coffee Company inspire you to take a closer look at your own communication vehicles and target audience. Yes, it's about great PR and marketing communications. It's also about having a great product, effective pricing, and seamless distribution. It's about understanding who you are and who you're trying to reach and then crafting messages that speak to your audience on a personal level.

BRAND MARKETING, REPUTATION MARKETING, AND BRAND CREATIVE

Brand marketing, reputation marketing, and brand creative are three important and interconnected elements of any company's overall marketing strategy.

- **Brand marketing** is how a company presents itself to the world, through everything from its logo, website, and advertising to its values, the user experience, and consumer interactions with its social media and owned media channels like blogs and newsletters.

- **Reputation marketing** is how a company interacts with employees, customers, and the world. It's all about managing and influencing consumer perceptions and highlighting the positive qualities of the brand.

- **Brand creative** involves creating a distinct brand identity through elements like logo design, color selection, packaging design, and web graphics.

So, brand marketing is about presenting a company's identity to the world, reputation marketing focuses on managing and influencing consumer perception, and brand creative deals with creating a unique and memorable identity. All three aspects work together to build a strong, cohesive brand image that resonates with consumers.

It's not a simple undertaking. It requires consistency and cohesion in and across your message, your product, and all communication channels—and the customer experience.

In this chapter, we'll discuss the importance of brand marketing, reputation marketing, and brand creative, especially in the modern media sphere. When you nail down what your brand is all about, you can dive into integrated marketing, spinning a yarn about your brand that not only sticks but also puts some distance between you and the competition.

AWARENESS OF BRAND, AWARENESS OF SELF

A former boss of mine years ago used to say, "Never believe your own PR." While a pretty simple phrase, it had deeper meaning—although it took me a while to understand what that meaning was. What he meant was that, both personally and professionally, it's important to not fall into an ego-driven feedback loop telling yourself how great you are. Professional communicators in particular need to be very aware of the messages they're sending to clients and the public.

That awareness needs to be aligned with your audience's needs and interests.

We have clients who call us regularly with requests such as, "Hey, we're coming up on our company's twentieth anniversary—let's get a press release out there." They think that's a big deal. So, we have a tough conversation to help them understand that, outside their organization, nobody really cares. It's not news. Customers certainly don't care. People are inherently kind of selfish. What they care about is "What are you going to do for me? How does this improve my life, my experience, or my day?"

Before you start deciding to put out that press release about your anniversary or post random self-important stuff on social media, take a moment of silence and introspection. Think about who your company is, what your brand represents, and what you're offering to your customers and the community. What are you trying to say, and what are you trying to offer to the world at large?

CASE STUDY: BUD LIGHT'S PARTNERSHIP WITH DYLAN MULVANEY

In early 2023, Bud Light partnered with Dylan Mulvaney, a transgender influencer, for a social media promotion. Now, Dylan is popular, with 1.8 million followers on Instagram and over 10.6 million on TikTok. But when she posted a video promoting a Bud Light contest, it led to a massive backlash from Bud Light's customer base, including calls for a boycott. Some of the most prominent voices supporting the boycott were people who had attacked the transgender community in the past, like musician Kid Rock, who even posted a video of himself shooting a stack of Bud Light cases. The controversy didn't stop there. Country singer Garth Brooks faced criticism when he said his new bar in Nashville would serve Bud Light, and he later acknowledged that his remarks caused "a little bit of a stir."[7]

Bud Light's VP of marketing at the time, Alissa Heinerscheid, did a podcast interview to discuss her vision for the brand and the need for inclusivity. She acknowledged that Bud Light had been in decline for a long time and needed to attract young drinkers to secure its future. Her goal: to move away from the "fratty, kind of out-

---

7   "Bud Light Faces Boycott Threat over Remarks on Gay Pride," *New York Times*, accessed February 8, 2024, https://www.nytimes.com/article/bud-light-boycott. html#:~:text=In%20June%2C%20Garth%20Brooks%20was,little%20bit%20of%20a%20 stir.%E2%80%9D.

of-touch humor" that had previously characterized the brand. She stressed the importance of representation and inclusivity in the brand's evolution, saying that people need to see others who reflect them in brand messaging. She believed that having a campaign that appeals to both women and men and feels lighter, brighter, and different would help achieve this goal.[8]

But, despite Heinerscheid's certainly good intentions to help Bud Light evolve and grow, the partnership with Mulvaney resulted in negative consequences for the brand's sales and reputation. And the loss of her job—she left the company in June 2023 after being placed on a leave of absence. Anheuser-Busch's VP overseeing marketing for mainstream brands was also placed on leave.[9]

The fallout from this campaign was significant. Bud Light's retail sales dropped, falling as much as 42 percent in some US metro areas. The beer also lost its top spot at bars and restaurants, falling to fourth place behind Miller Lite, Michelob Ultra, and Coors Light. Anheuser-Busch, the company behind Bud Light, even had to put some marketing executives on leave and announce layoffs in its corporate offices.[10]

So, what can we learn from this? It's a prime example of why it's crucial to understand your audience and the potential impact of your PR campaigns. If you make a product that is beloved by a very specific demo, then you'd better either embrace that demo or be prepared to

8   "Bud Light's Marketing VP Was Inspired to Update Fratty, Out-of-Touch Branding," *New York Post*, April 10, 2023, https://nypost.com/2023/04/10/bud-lights-marketing-vp-was-inspired-to-update-fratty-out-of-touch-branding/.

9   "Anheuser Executives Placed on Leave amidst Internal Investigation," CNN Business, April 24, 2023, https://www.cnn.com/2023/04/24/business/anheuser-execs-on-leave/index.html.

10   "Bud Light Sales Decline," *New York Times*, August 3, 2023, https://www.nytimes.com/2023/08/03/business/bud-light-sales-decline.html.

lose them if you're going to make a radical change. Know your brand. Know your audience. Be true to the core values of each.

Are your messages a true reflection of your company? Are they consistent? And, importantly, do they matter to your audience? Lack of awareness will cause a campaign to engage with the wrong people or across the wrong channels in the wrong ways. It's essential to take the time to understand who you are, both personally and professionally, and what your brand represents. By doing so, you'll be better equipped to create meaningful connections with your clients and the public, ultimately leading to more successful PR campaigns.

GOOD DISTRIBUTION, A QUALITY UX, AND A GOOD PRODUCT

Something that we talk a lot about internally and with clients is that, in the world of PR and marketing, good PR won't fix a bad business, and good marketing won't fix a broken one. You could have reams of PR, you could have huge amounts of earned media coverage, you could have the most viral social media campaigns on the planet, but if you can't get your product or service to the consumer, none of that matters.

Peter Thiel, a tech entrepreneur, a cofounder of PayPal, and part of the so-called "PayPal Mafia," encouraged business owners to think of distribution as something essential to their businesses. He emphasized that superior sales and distribution can create a monopoly even with no product differentiation, but the opposite is not true. In the old days, you could have the best peanut butter in the world, but if it wasn't in every supermarket in America, you weren't going to sell it because there was no other way for people to buy it. Well now, anyone with a little bit of time on a platform can build out a Shopify site or a WooCommerce site and start selling.

Distribution, as Thiel points out, is everything.

Take Apple, for example. After cofounding the company in 1976, Jobs eventually was pushed out by his board in 1985, and after a decade of declining sales, the diminished company brought him back in 1996. When he returned to the company, he focused on creating great products, great marketing, and great distribution. The Apple Store was as important as the iMac, iPad, and iPhone. Jobs understood that a strong distribution plan was crucial to the success of the brand, because the stores *were* the brand. From their clean open design, to naming the tech help desk a "genius bar," to the shirts employees wear, it's all designed to strike a balance between futuristic, approachable and slightly whimsical. You can't get that from products on display at Best Buy.

In the automotive industry, where we spend a lot of our time at my PR firm, the distribution model is incredibly important. You can do everything right on the marketing and PR front, but if the customer walks into a dealership and has a terrible experience, all your efforts are wasted.

So, even in a book about PR and marketing, it's worth emphasizing the importance of distribution. A strong distribution plan is integral to the success of your brand, and without it, even the most well-executed PR and marketing campaigns can fall flat.

HOW SEAMLESS DISTRIBUTION DRIVES CUSTOMER LOYALTY

A few years ago, I parted ways with a coffee brand that I really loved (sorry, another coffee story, but I drink a lot of the stuff). The brand was one of the first organic coffee roasters on the West Coast, and they had a good quality product, local cafés, and an online store. I was such a fan that I had a subscription for their coffee, going through about five pounds a week at my office and two pounds a week at my house.

And they managed to do the impossible with me as a consumer: They got me hooked on their product to the point where I just gave them my credit card and said, "You win. All you have to do is send me the product every month, and I'll smile and say thank you."

But they couldn't get the distribution process figured out. The product wouldn't ship, or they'd send the wrong thing, or they'd charge me for five pounds and send me one pound. After enough of these issues, I got so irritated that I canceled the subscription and switched to another brand—Black Rifle Coffee, actually.

This story illustrates the importance of making sure that every aspect of the customer experience is great. Even if you have a great product and a loyal customer base, if you can't deliver on the distribution side, you risk losing those customers. In my case, the coffee brand lost a loyal customer because they couldn't consistently deliver the product I wanted. So, it's crucial to ensure that your distribution channels are reliable and efficient to maintain customer satisfaction and loyalty.

THE IMPORTANCE OF KPIS AND MONITORING METRICS

KPIs (key performance indicators) and metrics are important tools for evaluating the effectiveness of your PR and marketing efforts. They provide quantifiable measures that can help you understand whether you're meeting your objectives and goals—and your customers' needs. Without them, you're basically driving without a map or any gauges to tell you how fast you're going, how far you have to go, and when you'll reach your destination.

For example, consider a situation where a customer has a problem with a product. The way you handle that situation—from the moment the customer contacts you to the resolution of their issues—can have a big impact on your brand's reputation. To measure these efforts, you might track metrics like the number of issues resolved on the first call, the average time to resolution, or customer satisfaction scores. These KPIs can give you valuable insights into the effectiveness of your customer service strategy.

But KPIs aren't just for customer service. You also need KPIs to measure and monitor your PR and marketing campaigns. Whether you're running a hyperlocal campaign or a nationwide—or global—campaign, you need to monitor results. This might involve tracking metrics like the number of new customers acquired, the increase in sales during the campaign, or the growth in brand awareness among your target audience.

Keep in mind that the metrics you choose will depend on your objectives (more about that in chapter 3). What's important, though, is that you're measuring something. In the end, as they say, "what gets measured, gets managed." When you're able to manage your PR and marketing efforts effectively, you're better positioned to build a strong, positive brand image. You'll understand your customers and their needs and interests, you'll understand how you stack up against the competition, and you'll continually have your eye on areas where you're either improving or losing ground.

Whether you're managing your own PR and marketing or working with an agency, you'll want to have reports that can help you understand how things are going. These should provide valuable and digestible information, not just a bunch of numbers, charts, and graphs.

For instance, at Kahn Media, we use Looker Studio (previously known as Google Data Studio) for data visualization and business intelligence. We customize dashboards for our clients to help them quickly and easily see their key KPIs to track campaign performance.

Regardless of the specific KPIs you monitor, ultimately, in addition to tracking leads and sales, you also want to track and maintain the stability of your brand.

INTEGRATED MARKETING AND MAINTAINING STABILITY IN YOUR BRAND VALUES

We talk a lot about integrated marketing, but what does that term really mean? Integrated marketing pulls together all the media channels—earned, owned, and paid—in a way that ensures consistency in messaging across those channels. They work in unison to communicate a brand's core values and messages to a specific audience. This requires a clear understanding of your brand, your company, your services and products, and the value you offer to your customers. It's crucial to be aware of what you're saying about yourself, what you're allowing to be said about you, and what you're putting out into the world.

But that doesn't always happen. Many companies either fail to realize the significance of this integrated approach or fail to execute on it; sometimes they even treat their marketing and PR efforts as an afterthought.

I've been saying this for years, and I'll continue to say it: There's this weird idea, especially with internal marketing and communications and PR teams at companies big and small, where social media management is treated as an afterthought. They think, "Well, let's just get some high school kid to do it," or, "Let's pay an intern to handle our social."

But here's the thing. Your social media is literally your primary window into your brand, your company, and your product or service. It's how you share who you are—how you convey your brand values. Why would you let some twenty-year-old who doesn't know about your company, doesn't care about your values, and is just looking for something to put on their résumé be in charge of that?

Think about it this way: If you owned a bank, would you let an underqualified twenty-year-old be the person in charge of handing out the money? It's probably not a good plan to make that person the loan officer. You should probably get someone who actually has a thorough understanding of the whole process and how it works.

So, the bottom line is that using interns to manage your social media isn't a good idea. Instead, invest in someone who truly understands your brand, your values, and your company's mission to effectively communicate with your audience and maintain a strong online presence.

That's true of all your messaging across earned, owned, and paid channels. Whether it's your blog, your newsletter, your social channels, earned media, and whether you're going out and doing PR or the press comes to you because of something you've done—whatever it is—whatever you communicate needs to be cohesive, consistent, and aligned. One of the greatest sins in both agencies and in-house marketing is relegating communication tasks to the cheapest body available, whether that body is in-house or at an agency. It's crucial to have people who genuinely care about your brand working on your brand. If they don't know, live, and care about your brand, they won't do a good job.

When you study brands that have been successful—like Black Rifle Coffee Company—whether they're working with one agency or many, whether they're using both internal and external resources—everything works together to communicate the core values of the brand and the core messages that are most relevant to a specific audience.

If you use a public relations firm, make sure you are involved in the planning process and that you are also responsive to the information gathered on your behalf. Clients need to be involved in the PR process. Integrated marketing is a team sport. A business in this process must actively bring drive, goals, honesty, and a clear mission to their campaigns. And you need to be an integral part of that.

You can sell great coffee to a niche market using crazy, even outrageous messaging, as long as it's brand supporting. You can't sell plain water to any audience using crazy, even outrageous messaging that's not brand supporting. And you can't sell anything if your product or service—and its distribution—doesn't live up to your messaging. You need to know who you are, and you need to be who you are—consistently, and across all channels, earned, owned, and paid.

Knowing yourself, your brand, and your product are foundational elements of any public relations campaign. Also of critical importance is learning about your customer, the recipient of all your hard work and effort. Often, getting their eyeballs is just the beginning of a strong strategy. One that requires a clear understanding of who they are and what they value.

TAKEAWAYS

→ What is your brand identity? What products, services, and their traits are essential for supporting this identity across all the places your audience interacts with your brand?

→ How would you describe your ideal customer? Create a profile including demographic details, interests, and values. Thoroughly understanding your target audience can help you do a better job of choosing media (earned, owned, and paid) and creating messages to influence them.

→ How has your brand identity manifested through your owned, earned, and paid communication channels? Do your messages align with the interests and values of your target audience?

→ Is your messaging consistent with who you really are and the customer experience?

CHAPTER 3

YOUR PIT STOPS AND DESTINATION

(YOUR PARTNERS AND AUDIENCE)

When it comes to PR in the digital environment, few names have reached as much prominence as MrBeast, a name that has become synonymous with YouTube influencers. If you're not familiar with MrBeast— here's a bit of background.

MrBeast, whose real name is Jimmy Donaldson, is known for pioneering a genre of YouTube videos focused on extravagant stunts, challenges, and philanthropy. His is the most followed account on YouTube, reaching 200 million subscribers in late 2023.[11] His most recent video at the time—*$1 vs $100,000,000 House*—broke the record for the most views in a twenty-four-hour time frame.[12] His journey to building the MrBeast brand is a master class in understanding and connecting with an audience and creating strategic partnerships to fast-track commercial success. It's a perfect opening for this chapter.

Donaldson is a content creator, but he doesn't just create content—he creates experiences for his audience. He understands the importance of personalization and novelty in the digital age. And he knows how to use partnerships to expand his brand to reach a larger audience (like MrBeast Burger, a virtual restaurant he started in late 2020 during the COVID-19 pandemic). At that time, I started seeing restaurants pop up on delivery services like GrubHub or DoorDash that I didn't recognize—the MrBeast Burger was one of them.

My wife and I tried it. It was great. I told my coworkers about it, and we'd order food and track where the deliveries were coming from. What we discovered is that the orders weren't coming from MrBeast Burger, they were coming from Red Robin. Red Robin turned out to be one of the virtual company's main partners.

You see, MrBeast didn't actually make the burgers or own the restaurants that sold them. As I dug into this more deeply, I learned that he used a "ghost kitchen" approach, leveraging the capabilities of existing restaurants like Red Robin, benefitting from their already established infrastructure, supply chain, and production capabilities.

11   "MrBeast Breaks YouTube Subscriber Milestone," GameRant, October 15, 2023, https://gamerant.com/mrbeast-youtube-subscriber-milestone/.

12   "YouTube Giant MrBeast Surpasses 200M Subscribers, Breaks His Own 24-Hour View Record," Nasdaq, October 16, 2023, https://www.nasdaq.com/articles/youtube-giant-mrbeast-surpasses-200m-subscribers-breaks-his-own-24-hour-view-record-and?time=1697505532#:~:text=His%20video%2C%20%E2%80%9C%241%20Vs%20%24100%2C000%2C000%2CDays%20Stranded%20at%20Sea%E2%80%9D%20video.

This allowed MrBeast to focus on the marketing end of the business. It was a perfect business model during the pandemic when restaurants were closed, and delivery became a popular option. Most Red Robin locations were in malls, which were also shut down during the pandemic, so it was a win-win for both parties.

As life started to open back up, though, MrBeast Burger faced some quality issues and started to get some blowbacks from customers. Donaldson didn't just ignore the issues. He publicly acknowledged and apologized for them, demonstrating his commitment to his brand—and his audience.

He didn't stop at burgers. He also launched Feastables, a brand of high-quality chocolate bars. He introduced the Bar, available in three flavors, with a massive sweepstakes offering more than one million dollars in prizes. Here again, he ran into quality issues, but he leveraged his audience to address them. When he learned that Bar fans loved the product but felt the point-of-purchase displays were a mess, he mobilized his fan base to help. He said, "Hey, I need you guys to go to your local Walmart, look for Feastables, and, if the display is messed up, fix it and take pictures and send them to me." He augmented the ask with a contest.

Brilliant! MrBeast used his rabid fans as merchandising employees—and virtual brand advocates. In essence, he inverted the traditional business model where you have a product or service, and you go out to look for an audience. He had an audience and he found products to drop into the funnel, leveraging his audience as part of his PR strategy. He determined, "If I'm true to who I am, and if I offer a great product, I already have an audience." So, he set out to build stronger relationships with that audience through new products, clever contests, and a constant stream of on-point and edgy communications.

It's a model for success in modern integrated marketing and PR that requires a thorough understanding of a specific audience and can be boosted through strategic partnerships that can provide value that you couldn't provide on your own.

INTEGRATED MARKETING AND EFFECTIVE MODERN PR FORGES RELATIONSHIPS WITH CUSTOMERS

The modern world of integrated marketing and effective PR has evolved significantly over the past several years. It's no longer about just selling a product or service but about building relationships with customers—and others.

The first step in doing that is finding overlaps in interest. The MrBeast example illustrates this well. He recognized that his audience had needs that overlapped the content he was providing with other needs—like the need to get good food during the pandemic, or to discover a truly tasty and carefully positioned candy bar. MrBeast's needs also overlapped with his partners'. He needed a way to engage with and build his audience—they needed, especially in Red Robin's case, the ability to remain viable and in business during the pandemic.

In both cases, those relationships need to provide mutual benefit, which they accomplished.

Remember, though, that despite MrBeast's massive following, effective integrated marketing isn't about trying to convert the masses. Instead, it's focused on finding specific customers with specific needs that you can uniquely fill. Integrated marketing aggressively finds an audience by becoming an active part of their "ecological niche"—the space they inhabit—within their industry.

Choosing the right social platforms is critical. Social channels give customers a chance to be part of the brand story and to make the brand part of their lives in a way that's not only relevant but also mutually beneficial. It's important, though, to not overinvest in a single platform. Platforms can change their fundamental rules and reach, making brands vulnerable if they're too focused on any one channel.

The value of integrated marketing is its integration—using a wide range of communication channels, both traditional and digital, to connect with and engage an audience. To build relationships in relevant and meaningful ways.

That can benefit from two things: creating friction and being authentic.

FRICTION AND AUTHENTICITY

In the world of marketing and PR, we often talk about reducing friction for consumers, making things as easy as possible for them to buy our products and services. But sometimes, a little friction can be a good thing—friction can create memorable moments that bring people together and create a shared experience.

In his book *Let My People Go Surfing*,[13] Yvon Chouinard, an alpinist and founder and co-owner of Patagonia, talks about the concept of yarak from falconry. Yarak is a state where the falcon is just hungry enough to be ultra-alert, on edge, and ready to hunt, but not so hungry that it's weakened. Yarak is used in falconry to keep the falcons always ready to hunt and in peak condition.

It's a concept that can also be applied to running a business successfully, and it's really stuck with me. In the business environment and setting, yarak is about keeping your company just hungry enough that you're really alert and on edge and looking for the next oppor-

---

13 Yvon Chouinard, *Let My People Go Surfing: The Education of a Reluctant Business-man* (Penguin Books, 2006).

tunity—you're not fat and lazy, and you're also not so hungry that you're weakened.

We might think of this as friction. As a business leader, you want to maintain enough friction that everybody stays engaged and alert and looking for that next opportunity. But not so much that they become overwhelmed or burned out.

This same thinking can apply to consumers and customers as well. When customer experiences are authentic and have just the right amount of friction, they become memorable—and they drive and build brand connections.

This idea really struck me not long ago when I was at an outdoor industry trade show in the booth of a company that makes high-end, European birdwatching binoculars that make you feel like you're right next to the bird, even if it's a mile away. This company had spent massive amounts of money to recreate the great outdoors in the convention center. They had artificial turf, fake campfires, Adirondack chairs, even elevation changes in the booth. And they had an upper viewing area where you could look down on their fake outdoor setting using their spotting scopes and binoculars.

So, there I was, standing in this booth, looking through a $3,000 pair of binoculars at someone else's booth on the other side of the trade show, and I couldn't help but think, "Man, they're spending a lot of money to have this really artificial experience." Creating meaningful integrated relationships requires more than that. As I was immersed in this trade show experience, it occurred to me that, maybe when we're creating experiences for our audiences, we need to not only create some intimacy in these experiences, but we also need to inject a little bit of friction.

That's exactly what we did with our TREAD Agency Traction Series Backcountry Summit, an experiential event that we put together, pairing high-profile outdoor brands with creators and journalists to talk, bond, go on an adventure together, and learn some new skills and connect through shared experience. Plus, it allowed us to test outdoor gear in the place it was designed to be used—outdoors. The inaugural summit featured lessons and talks from outdoor education thought leaders, including Creighton Greene of SCOUTE Arms, Laura Zerra from Carbon TV's *Decivilized*, Alaskan guide and owner of Outfitter Services Caleb Stillians, US Fish and Wildlife grizzly bear specialist Amber Kornak, Jordan Jones from the television show *Alone*, and Julie McQueen of Carbon TV.

We gathered these thought leaders with members of the media, outdoor brands, and participants together on a piece of land way off the grid in Montana near White Sulphur Springs. It is so off the grid, in fact, that we had five flat tires on three vehicles just getting there.

We spent the day climbing up this mountain, starting at around five thousand feet. I'm in pretty good shape, but, let me tell you, by the time we got to the top of that mountain, I thought I was going to die. Then we made camp at the top. We were all exhausted and starving, but we all also had this sense of accomplishment. We sat around the campfire, ate a great meal together, and had some of the best conversations I've ever had. There was no Wi-Fi, no phone service, no connectivity. We were all forced to be present and to engage with each other after a day of learning new things and overcoming challenges. The next day we made cowboy coffee over the campfire. Everybody was in a great mood, chatting and laughing. We even had a guy playing guitar.

It was the kind of experience that you just don't get from a traditional trade show or Zoom conference call.

We created camaraderie—and we invoked yarak.

Participants were put in a situation that required them to be alert and ready to seize opportunities, much like a falcon in the state of yarak. The experience was designed to be challenging, pushing participants to their limits while also providing them with a unique and memorable experience. Participants had to be hungry enough to seize the opportunity to learn new skills and connect with others, but not so hungry that they overextended themselves or became overwhelmed.

The event was impactful, and it's proven to have long-lasting impacts as well. We've held another event since then and plan to do more. It's a great way to personally connect with an audience in an environment where they're challenged and introduced to new things (products and ideas) and new people.

Before we can talk about identifying an audience and their needs, we need to talk about setting clear goals and benchmarks—defining the win. This isn't about just going out there and doing fun stuff or creating crazy events or stunts. It's activity with a purpose focused on clear goals and benchmarks and a clear understanding of your audience.

SETTING CLEAR GOALS AND BENCHMARKS

In the world of business, setting clear goals and benchmarks is akin to defining the win. It's about knowing where you're headed and how you'll know when you've arrived. This is where key performance indicators (KPIs) come into play. They are the road signs that guide you on your journey, telling you how far you've come and how far you still have to go.

The first step in setting clear goals and benchmarks is defining the win. What does success look like for you? For some, it might be increasing sales, but what does that mean exactly? Is it about market share? Are you trying to take market share from a competitor? Are you trying to increase your proportion of direct sales versus sales to distributors? Or maybe it's about profitability. Some companies become very focused on something like EBITDA (earnings before interest, taxes, depreciation, and amortization) and net profit. You can dramatically increase net profit and actually not increase your top-line sales. That's not even a marketing function at that point. That's an accounting, management, and supply chain function.

Your win won't look like others' wins. It's your win. Once you've defined what it is, you need to figure out what your KPIs are. These are the indicators that will tell you how close you are to your destination. They are the mile markers on your journey.

That journey doesn't stop, though, with defining your KPIs. You need to constantly check in on them and communicate about them with your team. This isn't a one-time meeting where everyone goes off and does their thing. These mile markers and the defined win need to be constantly revisited and discussed.

And you need to make sure that you're tying in the key leadership and operational components of your organization to your PR and integrated marketing efforts. You need to make sure that you're operationally ready to actually fulfill all the orders you'll be getting in after you've done a great job of creating demand. This will involve having a road map that outlines all the steps you need to take to reach your goal. It's a road map that will need to be constantly updated and adjusted as you make progress toward your goal.

Communication is key in this process. Everyone on the team needs to be aware of the successes and challenges the other teams are facing. If there's a delay, everyone needs to know about it. All areas of your organization—from marketing to sales to distribution to service—need to be working together to achieve your win. Your KPIs help you determine whether, and how well, that's taking place.

Once you know where you're going and you've defined the win, you can begin thinking about ways to reach out to specific market segments who are likely to want what you have to offer and to build relationships with those people. These are the tactical things that need to be done—what do the mile markers along the way look like on your road map? These are the tasks you need to accomplish to reach your win. So now you have to actually do the work. That starts with understanding your audience and your competition.

UNDERSTANDING YOUR AUDIENCE

In the world of PR and integrated marketing, understanding your audience is critical—not just knowing who they are, but also understanding their fears, their desires, and their needs. This understanding helps you align your brand with your audience and create messaging that resonates with them.

Back in the day, there was a lot of focus on creating personas. You'd do some market research to figure out "Who is our current customer? What is our ideal customer?" You'd then get into great detail about that specific persona. "This is Chris. Chris lives in the Midwest, is fifty-eight years old, has a college degree." You'd build that out with a lot of additional demographic and psychographic information, and you'd even have a picture or avatar of Chris.

Demographic information includes details like sex, race, age, geography, income, education. Psychographic information is more about how the customer thinks, what's important to them. Both types of information can be obtained through market research firms and trade associations—even through your own website these days. It used to involve a lot of guesswork. These days, though, we can really drill down into who our customers are, how they think, and what's important to them.

That focus on the image or avatar is important. We actually had a client with a very scientific marketing background that hired a market research firm to conduct demographic and psychographic research on their target audience, including focus groups. This was a company that sold very high-end luxury vehicles, so they could afford the investment, and it made sense given the price point of their products. The client then actually went out and bought full-size cardboard cutouts of an elderly couple and put them in the middle of his offices—they had their arms around each other, resembling your typical grandma and grandpa characters. That, at the time, was his target audience.

Not every company is selling a product at that price point; not every company can afford expensive research. But there are other things you can do. If you have a sales team, you can go talk to them— they're the ones actually interfacing with your customers. You might talk to employees in your customer service department. If you have a retail store, talk to people who work at the front counter. Do your own observation—show up and see things with your own eyes and make notes. You can reach out to your customers with quick polls. You can read customer reviews. There are a lot of ways that you can gather really great information about your customers.

How do they make decisions about purchasing what you have to offer? What kind of content are they consuming? Where do they spend their time? What brand values matter to them? What other values do they have—do they care that your product is made in America? Maybe it does; maybe it doesn't. But you need to know.

This information and in-depth knowledge about your customers can help you communicate with them in more impactful and appropriate ways.

We had a client, for example, that was a high-end luxury car company. When the COVID-19 pandemic hit, the company was unsure of how to interact with customers and potential customers. They didn't want to get it wrong or offend anyone. How do we talk to our customers about what's happening? Or do we not even address it? So, we did an extensive survey of their existing customers and a survey of their potential customers. We called about twenty of their top dealers and asked what they were hearing from customers. We asked what they and their employees were thinking. And we did a lot of best-practice research based on what other industries and other companies in their industry were doing.

The insights we gathered were invaluable. We found that people were scared and probably not going to make big purchase decisions for a while. Even so, they wanted to know that any brand they were considering or that they had purchased from was safety conscious—that they cared about them and their health, and the health and safety of their employees. And they wanted to feel seen and heard. They didn't want to be overlooked or forgotten about.

So, we crafted our messaging around these insights. We made sure that the brand didn't alienate its customers but instead made them feel valued and understood.

This approach to understanding the audience isn't just applicable in times of crisis. It's a process that can give you a competitive advantage in any situation. If you know what matters to your audience, you can make internal organizational changes and communicate those changes as features or benefits to your company and its products or services. And you can make changes to your messaging.

There are various ways to gather this information. You can conduct surveys. You can reach out directly to your customer base. You can even hire dedicated market research firms. The approach you take, and the depth of your research, will depend on your marketing budget. But you need to come up with ways of keeping a pulse of your audience so you understand them and can communicate with them effectively and deliver what they want and how they want it.

In addition to understanding your customers and potential customers, it's also important to understand your competition. You need to be prepared to convince your customers that what you have to offer is better.

UNDERSTANDING YOUR COMPETITION

When you're running a business, it's easy to get caught up in your own vision and forget to look around. It's like wearing blinders, staying in your lane, and ignoring the rest of the race. But understanding your competition is crucial. Not because you're going to copy them or follow in their wake, but so you can learn from their successes and failures and use that knowledge to differentiate your product and make it stand out.

Let's take a look at a real-life example. In chapter 2, we talked about the Bud Light incident where a transgender influencer was used for a failed social media promotion. It was a minor influencer engagement, but it had a massive impact—and not a good one. Budweiser, one of the biggest companies in its space, lost a significant chunk of market share due to a relatively small marketing spend. Now, if you were in the shoes of Miller or Coors, watching this unfold, you'd probably learn something from the situation—and you'd probably decide not to go there yourself, but to stay true to your brand and your market's values, playing it safe and maybe sponsoring NASCAR. Or, if you wanted to be daring, you might decide to lean into it and not shy away.

So, how do you go about understanding your competition? Start by looking at what they're doing. What are they saying? How do they describe themselves? How do they engage with their customers? What does their branding look like? Do you think they're doing a good job? Why or why not? What your competition is doing can help inform your own strategy—not to copy them, but to be different in meaningful ways from them to better engage your audience.

Understanding your competition is about positioning your brand in ways that will positively impact your audience—you have to understand your audience and your competition. Then you use that knowledge to make your product stand out. So, take off those blinders and start paying attention. You might be surprised at what you learn.

BRINGING PEOPLE TOGETHER BY BUILDING RELATIONSHIPS

Keep in mind that when we're talking about audience, we're not just talking about prospects or customers. There are other key audiences that you will need to build relationships with to achieve your KPIs. Successful integrated marketing involves forging relationships not only with customers but also with journalists, writers, content creators, influencers, and others who have an interest—or potential interest—in your products or services. Or who can help to influence your end user audience. In the automobile industry, for instance, dealers play a very influential role, so you need to understand them and build relationships with them.

Once you've identified and developed an understanding of those you want to build relationships with, the next step is to think about how you're going to come up with a novel approach to an existing problem they have. If you can solve a problem in a different way—like MrBeast did—you're going to get market share. But, if you're just doing things the same way as all your competitors are, there's no differentiation.

So how do you come up with a new model?

Let's look at a few additional examples to illustrate how this can be done.

The first example, the "Creator Clash," was put together by a group of YouTubers who truly understood their audiences and used that knowledge to create an opportunity that was not only meaningful but profitable. The group was led by YouTube personalities Ian Kane Jomha, known online as iDubbbz, who became popular through his Content Cop series, and Mikhail Varshavski, or Doctor Mike, known for his medical and health-related content.

They may seem like an unlikely pair. But what they had in common was an interest in combat sports. They decided to create a friendly competition among their audiences by staging a multimillion dollar pay-per-view charity event based on competition between content creators who also had an interest in boxing—either as participants or observers.

iDubbbz and Doctor Mike recognized that, in traditional fighting matches, the promoter usually makes the most money. They wanted to change that model, taking the promoter out of the mix. So, they decided to stage their own series of matches between content creators, promoting the event through the social channels of everyone involved and using a pay-per-view model. Funds raised were redirected back to the creators and donated to various charities.

Their initial Creator Clash event took place on May 14, 2022, at the Yuengling Center at the University of South Florida in Tampa. It was a huge success, with ten thousand fans in attendance and raising almost $1 million. They had successfully cut out the intermediary—fight promoters—to leverage their own audiences. Content had a role, but this wasn't just about creating content—it was about creating experiences that had friction and authenticity.[14]

Cleetus McFarland offers another example. Cleetus, whose real name is Garrett Mitchell, started out with a parody channel on YouTube, a sort of loving sendup of NASCAR culture. He built a huge following with his burnout videos and monster trucks and even bought his own racetrack in Florida, turning it into a platform to launch his own racing series.

What's really fascinating about what Cleetus did is that he's not just getting other YouTubers to race in his series—he's getting actual race car drivers to participate as well. They race in old Ford Crown Victorias, like taxi cabs and police cars. It's real racing, but with a tongue-in-cheek twist. And—here's the great part—he's getting more views on these races than actual race events like SCCA and IMSA races are getting.

Again, one of the keys to success is authenticity. If you can be super authentic, and you can reach out directly to your audience, you can build a loyal following—one that extends even beyond the event. Friction is also involved.

That's true of our Traction Series events too. We also wanted to maintain that momentum and connections after the event. So, we did a number of things to keep the conversations going—and to spread them to other audiences.

For example, we had our own crew along to film and capture the events and interactions. At the end of the event, we gave all that content to the sponsors and the creators, making it as easy as

---

14   "Creator Clash Boxing Event Debut Makes History with Sold-Out Arena and Over 100K Pay-Per-Views and Counting," Frontproof Media, June 14, 2024, https://www.frontproofmedia.com/boxing/creator-clash-boxing-event-debut-makes-history-with-sold-out-arena-and-over-100k-pay-per-views-and-counting.

possible for them to share it with their own audiences. We followed up postevent with a recap where we gave everyone each other's contact information and encouraged them to connect and talk. And we made it possible for brands to pitch every one of our influencers and content creators and journalists if they wanted to. Then we left the communication channels open. We created group chats on WhatsApp and just let them keep going. The cool thing is that I'm still getting notifications daily that those group chats continue to be active, months later.

The way we connect with our audiences and help them connect with each other as marketers today has really evolved. It's no longer about just selling a product or service, but about building relationships and creating experiences. We've found that curating these experiences allows people to forge meaningful relationships. With our Summits, we provide all the logistical support. We curate the guests, the media, the content creators, the sponsors, and the subject matter experts. We loosely script the chain of events to ensure people have content to cover, that they stay engaged, but that they also have time to network. We provide good food and even a place for people to unwind with a cold beer if they want to.

We take the message, and the event, directly to our audience. But while we—and MrBeast, iDubbbz, Doctor Mike, Cleetus, and others—have successfully bypassed the intermediaries, we don't entirely ignore the intermediaries. We brought the intermediaries along for the ride, together with their own audiences, and made it not only possible, but easy, for them to interact with each other. That creates value for everyone involved.

These new ways of creating partnerships to drive better audience interactions augment rather than replace traditional marketing practices. Do trade shows provide value? Of course they do. It's not an either/or proposition. Today's marketers can integrate traditional and digital, large-scale, and more intimate events. They can rely on third-party intermediaries sometimes. They can go directly to their audience(s) other times. They can bring all these groups together. And, if they can do that authentically, introducing just a bit of friction to the process, they can achieve measurable, and often remarkable, results.

But, while the examples we've been looking at are clever, fun, and entertaining, it's important to point out that this isn't just about being clever, fun, and entertaining. Ultimately, it's about achieving some desired results.

KNOW WHERE YOU'RE GOING (GOALS AND KPIS)

We've talked about identifying your win and determining the KPIs you'll monitor. It's always been important to know where you're going—your marketing goals—and to track and be able to report on whether you're getting there. In the old days, though, that involved a lot of smoke and mirrors, really scrambling to convey to your clients that you were achieving some level of success. We've talked about the old "heavy binders full of clips" method and measuring success based on the thud the binder makes when dropped on a desk. But judging PR effectiveness by the weight of clips attained isn't a meaningful metric of success.

Fortunately, in today's digital environment we have the ability to do a better job. The way we track KPIs and metrics has really evolved and continues to evolve. For instance, we've moved away from the old days of Google Analytics, which was great for its time, to the ability to see the bigger picture by bringing in data from different platforms.

That's what we do with our clients. Using Looker Studio, a free tool from Google that used to be called Google Data Studio, we build dashboards for our clients that bring in application program interfaces (APIs) from other platforms. So now we're not just looking at their own website data, we're bringing in data from Facebook, Instagram, YouTube, search, and a variety of other different plug-ins and tools depending on their specific situations and measurement needs.

With Looker Studio, we can see how people are interacting with their content. We can see site traffic, and we can see how that site traffic converts. We can even bring in data from paid search and paid social, on top of all the organic social content and all the organic traffic referral and search engine optimization (SEO) and site data.

And it's all visualized to make it easier to consume and to understand.

Building these dashboards does take time, but the only cost for anyone, whether it's an in-house marketer or an agency, is the time to do it. And the value it provides is immense. It gives us a comprehensive view of our performance across all platforms, and it allows us to make data-driven decisions that can really move the needle for our clients.

I'll admit, though, that our clients have mixed reactions to this. Most love it. But a few get a bit scared—usually those who aren't that technologically proficient. They just think It's too much information. But the great thing is that we can provide whatever level of analysis in whatever way they prefer to see it. Those who want more detail can have it. For those who don't, we can prepare an executive summary with just the top-line numbers. It's important to point out that our clients' level of interest, or fear, has nothing to do with what generation they're from—we have clients in their seventies who will spend hours going through these reports once a month and clients in their twenties who say, "Just give me six sentences on where we're at."

The shift to digital has allowed us to give clients exactly what they want and how often they want it. What's especially cool, though, is that we're at this integration point where we can pull together all these different data points and provide an indication of how everything we're doing across all these different channels is working. Are the numbers going up, or down? What's the cost per customer acquisition? What's the cost per click? What's the conversion rate?

And, it's completely free of monetary cost! There was a point not that long ago where you'd have to pay a company like McKinsey hundreds of thousands, if not millions of dollars, to get this kind of data. Today, it's all right there, and it's all free—but the value you get out of it is about how much time you're willing to put in.

Compared to the "thud factor" of my early days in the business, we've come a long way. Do we definitively have the ability to draw a straight line between the content that caused a customer to take a specific action? No, it's still hard to draw that line. But what we do have is the ability to take all these data inputs and paint a much clearer picture than we ever could before.

Effective public relations strategies require that a company (or individual) know themselves, their product/content, and their customers incredibly well. For the first time, the media landscape has the tools to do this on a level that makes this knowledge a two-way street. This discourse between the customer, the product, and an organization is the critical element that makes or breaks a PR campaign.

TAKEAWAYS

As you consider where and how you could build relationships to boost your integrated marketing efforts, ask yourself these questions:

→ Identify a segment of your audience that you haven't fully engaged with yet. Then develop a plan to create content or experiences that specifically target this segment, using MrBeast's approach as inspiration. Who are your best allies in your business ecosystem?

→ Think about your audience, or specific segments of your audience. What partnerships, contests, or unique digital experiences would align with both your brand values and the audience's interests?

→ Reflect on your past, current, or potential partnerships. How could these partnerships enhance your brand's reach, engagement, or impact?

→ Audit your recent marketing campaigns and customer interactions. Were your brand's core values communicated consistently and authentically across all channels? If not, develop an action plan to address the gaps or disconnects.

→ Think about your customer journey. Are there areas where introducing "friction" could actually enhance the customer experience and engagement, similar to our outdoor trade show example?

→ Review your current business goals and KPIs—do they effectively measure the impact of your outreach efforts? Set up a dashboard using tools like Looker Studio to monitor these metrics over time.

CHAPTER 4

THE FAST LANE OF D2C:

THE EVOLUTION OF CUSTOMER EXPERIENCE

Attention, interest, desire, action—or AIDA—used to be the holy grail for marketers. It's a model that described the process of capturing a customer. And the model worked well for a while. But modern marketers recognize that it doesn't go far enough. Today's marketing model extends beyond action—or that initial purchase—to encompass loyalty and advocacy. Brands that understand this and that can deliver an exceptional customer, and repeat customer, experience can stand out.

Here's an example from my own experience.

One year as we approached the holidays, despite the fact that my wife and I had agreed "no presents," I decided to get her something

69

anyway. So, I went to a store in the mall—Soma—and I asked if they had some really soft, really warm pajamas because she's often cold. And they did! And she loved them! In fact, she loved them so much that she was kind of wearing them out. So, when Valentine's Day rolled around, I thought, "Hey, why not get her another pair of those pajamas she really loves?" So, I went back to the store and said, "Hey, I'd like to buy another pair of pajamas, but I can't remember the exact size, product, or color I got before."

I'm not just any customer walking in. I'm a customer with a history. And, in this case, the brand delivered. They were able to pull up my previous purchase—they knew the product line, the color, the size, everything. But unfortunately, they didn't have those pajamas in stock.

Not to worry! They said, "We can order from our warehouse directly." So, I thought, "Okay, let's see how this goes." I completed the purchase and, because they already had my cell number from my previous purchase, as I was leaving the mall, my phone buzzed. It was an SMS from Soma thanking me for my purchase and promising to keep me up to date every step of the way. Which is exactly what they did. I continued to receive updates following the pattern of "Your order is being prepped," "Your order has shipped," "Your order is out for delivery," "Your order has been delivered." Every step of the way, they provided reassurance and kept me informed until the moment of truth—the product was delivered.

But the company didn't stop there. Once the product had been delivered and a brief amount of time had passed, they sent another message to ensure I was satisfied with the purchase and encouraging me to leave a review.

Soma, like other savvy brands, knows that it's not just selling a product. It's selling an experience. By leveraging their customer relationship management (CRM) system, they're able to provide a personalized service experience along with proactive communication at every step of the way. They're able to turn a simple purchase into a story worth sharing.

That's the power of data-driven customer experience. It's not just about the transaction; it's about building a relationship, fostering loyalty, and ultimately turning a happy customer into a brand advocate.

THE EVOLUTION OF D2C MARKETING

Direct-to-consumer, or D2C, marketing may seem like a twenty-first-century e-commerce phenomenon, but if you think about it, marketing started as a direct-to-consumer endeavor.

Back in the day, small family-owned businesses were the norm in most communities. More than just stores, they served as community hubs where people gathered to do business and to socialize. Shop owners likely knew most of their customers intimately, even without the modern benefit of CRM systems. From the 1700s through the early 1900s, these shops provided everything from dry goods to medicine and, like Cheers, shop owners knew their customers by name.

Then, as the economy evolved from agrarian to industrial and transportation revolutionized production and distribution of goods, the department store era emerged. Retailers like Aaron Montgomery Ward emerged with storefronts in larger cities and catalog sales offered to rural customers. Department stores and catalogs offered a collection of products from various brands, creating a barrier or third party between the brand and the end-user consumer.

Fast-forward to the digital age, and we experienced another revolutionary shift in how products are made available to consumers. Once again, brands have the opportunity to engage in direct-to-consumer sales interactions but now on a massive scale. E-commerce brands have the ability to, once again, connect directly with consumers while also gathering valuable customer data. They have the ability to "know" their customers on a first-name basis because of technology that makes that possible and allows them to capture, store, and leverage massive amounts of information. This ability has fueled the twenty-first-century version of D2C marketing.

It's not just about cutting out the middleman but about control over brand image, customer experience, and, most importantly, the data that can help brands better understand their customers. That allows for a more personal connection that is reshaping the retail landscape.

That control comes at a cost, of course. In a competitive landscape that is now global and massively online, the need to differentiate and establish trust with consumers is more critical than ever before.

The basics remain the same, though, despite the digital landscape and the endless choices that today's consumers have available to them. It's still really all about convenience, selection, a positive shopping experience, and value. But the marketing funnel has expanded in a D2C environment. Savvy marketers, and brands, recognize the need to provide exceptional value and service across the continuum from awareness to advocacy.

THE EVOLUTION OF THE MARKETING FUNNEL FROM A D2C POINT OF VIEW

The stages of the new marketing funnel—awareness, interest, desire, action, loyalty, and advocacy—are pillars of a successful D2C strategy. It's a journey from making potential customers aware of your brand to turning them into passionate advocates.

Awareness

Awareness is the first stage of the funnel, where potential customers learn of your brand's existence. In the traditional model, this was achieved through mass media advertising—TV, radio, and print ads. Today, the digital landscape offers a plethora of channels to create awareness. Social media platforms, search engines, online ads, and influencer partnerships are just a few of the ways to reach a broad audience.

Consider the case of the mattress company Casper. When it launched, it faced a significant challenge—how to make people aware of a brand that sold mattresses online. The company used a mix of PR, social media, and influencer marketing to create buzz. They sent mattresses to influencers, who shared their unboxing experiences and reviews on social media. They also used targeted online ads to reach potential customers who were searching for sleep-related products. This multichannel approach helped Casper quickly gain awareness in a crowded market.

Interest

Once potential customers are aware of your brand, the next step is to pique their interest. This stage involves engaging content that educates and informs, helping potential customers understand how your product or service can meet their needs or solve their problems.

Let's take a look at another D2C company, Glossier. Glossier, a beauty brand, excels in this stage by using content marketing to build interest. They create blog posts, videos, and social media content that not only showcases their products but also provides valuable beauty tips and tutorials. This content is tailored to their audience's interests and helps build a relationship with potential customers by offering value beyond the product itself.

Desire

Once you have a potential customer's interest, the next step is to build desire. This is where you showcase the unique benefits and features of your product or service, convincing potential customers that they need it.

Warby Parker, an eyewear company, is a great example of creating desire. It offers a unique home try-on program where customers can select five frames to try at home for free. This program not only removes the barrier to purchase but also creates a sense of exclusivity and personalization. By allowing customers to experience the product in their own environment, Warby Parker builds desire and makes it easier for customers to envision themselves using their product.

Action

The action stage is where potential customers become actual customers by making a purchase. In the traditional model, this was often the end goal. However, in the modern D2C model, this is just the beginning of the customer journey.

Harry's, a D2C shaving company, excels at converting interest and desire into action. They offer a seamless online shopping experience with a clear call to action, easy navigation, and multiple payment options. They also use retargeting ads to remind potential customers who have visited their site but haven't made a purchase. This combination of a smooth user experience and strategic follow-up helps convert browsers into buyers.

Loyalty

Loyalty is about creating repeat customers. It's achieved through exceptional customer service, consistent communication, and rewards for repeat purchases.

Dollar Shave Club, another D2C shaving company, has mastered customer loyalty. They provide a subscription service that delivers shaving products to customers' doors regularly. This convenience, combined with high-quality products and excellent customer service, keeps customers coming back. They also engage with customers through personalized emails and social media, making them feel valued and appreciated.

Advocacy

The final stage of the funnel is advocacy, where loyal customers become brand advocates. They promote your brand to others, providing valuable word-of-mouth marketing.

One of the best examples of advocacy in the D2C space is the carmaker Tesla. Tesla's customers are some of the most passionate advocates you'll find. The brand encourages this by creating a sense of community among owners. They host events, offer referral programs, and engage with customers on social media. This creates a network of enthusiastic advocates who actively promote Tesla to their friends and family.

DISTRIBUTION AND ITS ROLE IN D2C

Distribution is particularly critical in D2C marketing. Remember, the old AIDA model ended with action—the consumer makes a purchase decision. Customer satisfaction doesn't stop there, of course. In an e-commerce environment, many consumers are placing an order and then waiting to receive the product. Effectively handling distribution is a key element in generating loyalty.

Brands are realizing this and taking steps to ensure that every stage of the buyer journey is understood and managed to provide an exceptional experience. Dropping the ball at any stage can lead to dissatisfaction, which detracts from both loyalty and advocacy.

In the old days, you could have the best peanut butter in the world, but if it wasn't on every supermarket shelf in America, you might as well forget generating sustainable sales. No distribution. No sales. It was as simple as that. Today, though, things are different. Anyone with a laptop can set up a Shopify or WooCommerce site and begin selling directly to consumers. The barrier to entry has been lowered. That's a huge shift because it means that distribution is no longer about shelf space—it's about digital presence and reach.

Peter Thiel, cofounder of PayPal and author of *Zero to One*, perhaps said it best: You can have a mediocre product and great distribution and still be a market leader. The converse is not true. You could have the best product in the world, but without distribution, you're not going to generate sales. Distribution, Thiel asserts, must be part of product design.

In a D2C environment, distribution takes on new meaning. It's not just about getting your product out there; it's about creating a direct line to your customers. It's about building a relationship with them, understanding their needs, and delivering value straight to their doorstep, their inbox, or their smartphone screen.

When we talk about distribution in the modern D2C world, we're talking about a lot more than just logistics. We're talking about customer acquisition, retention, and ongoing engagement. We're talking about building a brand that lives in the pocket of every consumer with a smartphone. We're talking about turning customers into advocates who will sing your praises from the digital rooftops.

Distribution today isn't just about reaching customers—it's about resonating with them in ways that are so meaningful that they become rabid advocates for your brand. That shift, and the proliferation of digital channels to reach consumers, has had a massive impact on how brands use marketing and PR in a digital environment.

THE IMPACT OF D2C ON MARKETING, BRANDING, AND PR

One of the most profound changes brought about by D2C in the twenty-first century is the emphasis on authenticity and direct consumer engagement. As traditional media channels have become more and more decentralized, the role of independent content creators and influencers has become increasingly important (more about this in a later chapter). Brands are now leveraging these partnerships not just for their reach but also for their ability to convey authenticity and to drive genuine enthusiasm for the products they endorse.

Authenticity is crucial in storytelling. The alignment of values and communication strategies between brands and their partners can lead to win-win situations that drive sales and enhance loyalty.

The ability to engage in authentic relationships and conversations with consumers and customers isn't just important when selling a product or providing service—it's also important as many brands have discovered when navigating the kind of service breakdowns and crises that can challenge a brand's longevity, or even existence.

Influencers don't become influencers without authenticity and a deep and very accurate understanding of their audience. Even when influencers seem to be focused on the same type of brand, the nuances

in how they reach out to their audiences really illustrate the importance of niche targeting—and authenticity.

That was driven home to me recently when I was doing some
interviews for my podcast with two motorcycle content creators.
They're both female. They both ride motorcycles. They're both very
successful influencers. And yet two human beings could not be more
different!

One is Canadian, lives in California, and has more of a biker
image. She's hardcore, has tattoos, rides a chopper with no front
brakes that she takes across the country on crazy long-haul road trips.
She's built choppers and displayed them at shows. She started her
own apparel brand, which is also pretty hardcore. The other is from
South Florida, rides an import sport bike, does track days, and puts
out content ranging from tech and how-to videos to content that
looks pretty close to a fashion shoot. They're both making a living as
influencers, but in slightly different ways.

Becky Goebel is the Californian Canadian and she pretty much
embodies the spirit of hardcore 1970s chopper culture. Known for
her long-haul road trips on a hardtail, complete with tattoos and a
no-front-brake setup, Becky found herself on a serendipitous journey
into the influencer world. She was already building a name and a
reputation in the bike world by competing at shows like Born Free,
but a few viral posts on Instagram and TikTok catapulted her into
social media stardom, leading her to expand her presence to YouTube
and other platforms. Her revenue comes from promoting her own
merch line and from sponsorship deals with major brands like Harley-
Davidson and Bell Helmets.

The South Florida sport bike rider is known as Jess R1des. With
her model-like appearance and a penchant for high-speed Japanese
sport bikes, Jess specializes in content that primarily revolves around

her experiences with road racing and track days. Her presence spans multiple platforms, including TikTok, YouTube, and Instagram, where she shares her insights and passion for motorcycles. Her approach to influencer marketing is strategic and brand conscious. She engages in long-term partnerships with established brands. Preferring not to pursue payment for single posts, instead, she focuses on creating meaningful content that can make multiple impressions. Her affiliate deals, offering discount codes to her audience, not only provide value to her followers but also allow her to track the ROI of her sponsorships.

Both creators stressed that they handle much of their content creation solo, with little to no crews or editors, and both have a similar strategy of creating mostly vertical thirty-second video that can be deployed with minimal changes across Instagram as Reels, YouTube as Shorts, and on TikTok at the same time. Both also stressed that they have a commitment to authenticity, working only with brands they believe in.

They're different. They're authentic. They know their audiences, and they're committed to delivering content that continues to engage their audiences while also providing the opportunity to generate revenue. Their difference demonstrates that there is no one-size-fits-all approach to content creation or monetization. They've each successfully demonstrated their ability to carve out a unique niche within the motorcycle community, despite their different styles, by emphasizing authenticity that resonates with their audiences and builds trust—a crucial element, as we've seen, in influencer marketing.

A NEW NORMAL

It's fascinating how the PR and advertising landscape has evolved, especially with the rise of influencers like Becky and Jess. It's this wild, hybrid space that's not quite PR, not quite traditional advertising, but something entirely new and incredibly effective for those who get it right. It's all about that third-party endorsement component, which has always been the golden ticket in PR, particularly in the enthusiast space.

Imagine you're a tent company, and you get a glowing review in *Outside Magazine* or *Men's Journal.* That's a massive win. You get this huge earned media boost, potentially reaching millions, and suddenly everyone thinks, "Wow, that tent sounds awesome. I want to buy it." That kind of editorial feature can have a far greater impact than any ad could ever hope to achieve.

But what if your audience doesn't read those magazines? That's where advertising traditionally came in, offering guaranteed placement. You paid the money; they ran the ad. For decades, the best approach was a hybrid one: a mix of ads, PR, and owned media like catalogs, or, nowadays, websites and social channels. If you had all three of them, you were golden. This still holds true for D2C strategies.

But—getting that earned media in traditional outlets is getting tougher. The number of independent outlets is dwindling. Meanwhile, the opportunity to buy ads on social platforms is wide open—but so is the competition. You're not just competing with a few other tent companies; you're up against potentially dozens, all targeting the same look-alike audiences on Facebook, Instagram, or TikTok.

So how do you stand out? How do you drive consumers to your e-store to sell that product? It's all about relationship-based selling. Both Becky and Jess demonstrate how their brands work because of their authenticity and genuineness—they resonate with their audience; they share the same values.

It's a transparent, authentic conversation. It's the new PR/advertising hybrid.

CREATING LOYALTY AND ADVOCACY THROUGH EFFECTIVE D2C ENGAGEMENT

Brand managers and marketers have an opportunity today, as we've seen, to engage customers—and consumers—in direct conversations, to interact with them directly without the filter of third-party intervention, and to maintain those relationships over time. Doing so requires having a strong D2C communication strategy and being proactive in engaging with these audiences before, during, and after a sale has been made.

It's important to focus on the entire customer journey—not just the purchase. Using CRM tools to overcommunicate and make the sales and after-service process frictionless can set the stage for a positive experience. But that's just the beginning. After the purchase, it's important to continue to engage with customers through updates, delivery notifications, requests for reviews, and information on new products, services, or service offerings that they may find valuable. This is an approach that not only earns loyalty but also encourages customers to become advocates for your brand.

Technology plays an important role here. CRM systems can be utilized to automate communication and provide updates at every stage of a customer's interaction with you as I experienced when repurchasing Soma pajamas for my wife. This proactive approach keeps customers informed and engaged, ultimately building trust, loyalty, and advocacy.

Understanding the customer experience is important. If you don't know what that experience is—from purchase to advocacy—make an effort to find out. You may be surprised to learn that there are holes or gaps in this experience—or even major dissatisfiers that can thwart your most well-intentioned customer service efforts. Assess and ensure that every touch point with a customer is designed to exceed their expectations. Whether product quality, customer service, the purchasing process, or after-purchase follow-up, aim for excellence. Meeting—in fact, exceeding—expectations is key to maintaining customer loyalty and gaining their advocacy.

Don't overlook the importance of distribution in the D2C model. Keep in mind that a mediocre product with great distribution can still lead the market. You want an excellent product, of course, but the point here is that distribution matters. Don't overlook it.

Taking these steps will help you when everything is working smoothly for your brand. They will be even more important, though, as we'll see when things don't go so well. Strong relationships and advocacy will serve you not only when customers are delighted but also when they're dismayed.

With opportunity comes risk. Direct connection and engagement with your consumer and customer audiences offer opportunities to engage and delight them. These interactions aren't always smooth, though, and there are plenty of external forces that may thwart your best intentions. Proactivity and transparency are must-haves in this environment.

TAKEAWAYS

What steps could or should you take to leverage the potential for a D2C environment to help build loyalty and advocacy among your customers?

→ Reflect on whether your brand's narrative is genuine and designed to resonate with your audience's values and experiences. Are you walking the talk? Is the experience you promise the experience they receive?

→ Think about opportunities to engage customers postpurchase and turn them into brand advocates.

→ Consider how you could leverage technology tools and data to help personalize and optimize customer interactions to make each touch point memorable.

→ Evaluate your customer service, product distribution, and delivery processes to ensure that they meet or exceed customer expectations—even (in fact, especially) if there are other third-party partners involved.

→ Consider how a more concerted focus on D2C marketing could help you connect more directly—and authentically—with customers and gather valuable data.

CHAPTER 5

TRAFFIC PATTERNS

(ENGAGING WITH THE NEW DISCOURSE)

I n 2020, Chipotle agreed to pay a $25 million federal fine—at the time, the largest-ever fine of its kind—to settle criminal charges related to *E. coli* and norovirus outbreaks that occurred between 2015 and 2018. More than one thousand people were impacted through five separate foodborne illness outbreaks at restaurants in Los Angeles, Boston, Virginia, and Ohio, all caused by employees failing to follow food safety protocols.[15]

Chipotle's woes were widely known at the time and drew a sharp contrast between the fast-casual restaurant's positioning as a healthier

---

15   "Chipotle Mexican Grill Agrees to Pay $25 Million Fine and Enter a Deferred Prosecution Agreement to Resolve Charges Related to Foodborne Illness Outbreaks," US Department of Justice, February 3, 2024, https://www.justice.gov/opa/pr/chipotle-mexican-grill-agrees-pay-25-million-fine-and-enter-deferred-prosecution-agreement.

alternative to traditional fast food, with locally sourced ingredients and fair-trade practices. The scandal led to a decline in sales and damage to the company's reputation, as might be expected.

But that damage didn't last.

Fast-forward to today, and Chipotle is not only still in business but is thriving. While CNBC reported that Chipotle was struggling a year after the crisis, the restaurant chain weathered it well. In 2023, their shares rose almost 40 percent, according to the Motley Fool.[16]

THE POWER OF RADICAL TRANSPARENCY

How did Chipotle manage to come back after such a public catastrophe? Through radical transparency and direct engagement with its customers championed by the company's CEO, Steve Ells. Ells publicly apologized and took full ownership of the crisis. They were open and honest about the issues they faced and the steps they took to address them. They implemented new rigorous testing programs to ensure food safety and shared these initiatives with the public. They promoted their commitment to food safety and new safety initiatives through social media, TV commercials, online ads, and press releases. They also developed promotional events and rewards programs to incentivize consumers to give them another chance and to encourage brand loyalty among target groups.

By engaging directly with their customers and demonstrating their commitment to food safety, Chipotle was able to regain the trust of its customers and rebuild its reputation. It's an example of PR communicating truth, and that's powerful.

16   "3 Tasty New Reasons to Buy Chipotle Stock," Motley Fool, November 2, 2023, https://www.fool.com/investing/2023/11/02/3-tasty-new-reasons-to-buy-chipotle-stock/.

Here's another example that draws a sharp contrast between authenticity and transparency, and the kind of subterfuge that used to define PR practices.

Remember the story about the CEO of Ford from the first chapter of this book? The summer of 2023, Jim Farley decided to embark on a tour of California in the new electric version of the F-150, the Ford Lightning. The idea was simple: a victory lap to show off the prowess of this new electric beast. But as it turned out, the journey was anything but smooth. The truck itself wasn't the problem, but rather the infrastructure supporting it. Charging stations were few and far between, and even when they were available, the charging times were far from ideal. This was a problem not just for Farley, of course, but clearly for anybody considering buying this expensive vehicle. Even if the charging stations weren't Ford's fault, they still represented a barrier—and a reason not to buy.

But instead of brushing the problem under the rug, Farley chose a different path. He took to his social channels and did interviews, employing radical transparency. He admitted that things didn't go as planned and acknowledged the need for serious discussions about the infrastructure to support electric vehicles (EVs).

Now, let's contrast this with a similar situation involving Jennifer Granholm, the Secretary of Energy. Around the same time, she embarked on an EV road trip on the East Coast to promote infrastructure improvements and EVs. She faced the same issues as Farley, but her approach was different. In her case, her staff went to charging stations in advance, blocking off spots with internal combustion vehicles so that she wouldn't have to wait. This obviously resulted in massive inconvenience for other EV users who couldn't access the charging spots to charge their own vehicles. When the media picked up on this, her office didn't fully own up to the mistake, instead blaming it on the staffers.

Farley, on the other hand, was candid about his experience. He acknowledged the issues with the charging infrastructure and took responsibility for it. And he even went a step further, announcing that Ford was in talks with Tesla to adopt their superior charging technology, despite his previous criticisms of the company.

These two contrasting experiences highlight the importance of transparency and owning up to challenges. Farley's approach not only acknowledged the issues but also showed a commitment to finding solutions. This level of candor and transparency can be highly valuable when communicating with consumers.

Unfortunately, PR practices have historically not been entirely focused on transparency or truth. It's a profession that is often characterized by "spin"—taking a bad situation and positioning it in a positive way. Taking a bad product, service, distribution method, customer experience, etc., and explaining it away.

The profession was, in fact, designed to get the very results it often achieves—disillusionment and distrust. PR practitioners engaged with the media in an attempt to influence them to cover a story, or a product or service, in a favorable way. That model is eroding and giving way to a more direct and transparent discourse.

THE TRADITIONAL PR MODEL VERSUS TODAY'S

Imagine you're doing PR for a major hotel chain and you're about to open a new resort. You'd probably invite all the travel media to come and check it out. You'd fly them out, give them a first-class experience, cover their meals, and even arrange a meeting with the hotel's GM. They'd get the full experience, and then they'd go back and write about how great the property is. Sure, they might throw in a critique or two to seem honest, but they're not going to trash you. They want to be invited to the next big thing, and they don't want to upset the publicist who arranged everything.

This happens in other industries, too, like automotive and entertainment. I've been on both sides of the table—I've been the one writing the articles and the one doing PR. There's actually a very small group of people, maybe around 100 to 150, who get paid full time to write about cars. There are plenty of freelancers and people who write about cars as a side gig, but the number of full-time car journalists is pretty small.

These journalists usually write for automotive websites or magazines, and a few cover automotive for newspapers or news outlets. It's a strange business model because they're writing for specific outlets, and they need to maintain a good relationship with the companies they're writing about. They can't be too critical, or they risk losing access to new cars and industry events.

So, it's a bit of a balancing act. They need to be just critical enough to seem honest but not so much that they upset anyone.

Robert E. Peterson, a Hollywood publicist, played a significant role in establishing this model. After World War II, Peterson noticed a growing interest in cars among young men who had returned from the war with mechanical skills and a taste for adrenaline. He saw an opportunity in this trend and started *Hot Rod Magazine* in 1948, which became the first mainstream car enthusiast magazine. A year later, he started *MotorTrend*. Peterson's publishing company quickly grew into one of the biggest in America, rivaling even Hearst.

But it's a model that has its critics. Some argue that it creates a sycophantic relationship between the media and the industries they cover. Brands wine and dine the media in an attempt to get favorable coverage. Journalists, despite their acknowledged need to be unbiased, may be hesitant to provide truly critical coverage for fear of being blacklisted from future events. This can lead to a lack of objectivity in their reporting. Bias, of course, does exist in the world of PR.

It's a model that also doesn't allow for a great deal of discourse with an audience. There's no interaction. It's impersonal.

In recent years, this model has been disrupted by the rise of digital media and direct-to-consumer advertising. Brands can now produce their own content and engage directly with potential buyers, bypassing the need for third-party endorsement from journalists. Additionally, the rise of influencers and content creators such as mommy bloggers in the automotive space has further diversified the landscape.

Media relations and public relations, while interconnected, serve different purposes in a business's communication strategy. Media relations involves communicating with the consumer through the lens of the media, leveraging various media opportunities to convey messages. On the other hand, public relations deals directly with the public, managing the company's reputation and fostering positive relationships.

MEDIA RELATIONS

The traditional modality of media relations doesn't allow for much discourse with an audience or customer. Traditionally, press releases have been used to reach out to the media in the hope that they will cover your story. The media are in the middle—between your company's story and your audience. And they're one part of the process. But a press release really won't resonate—even if it's impeccably written, following AP style and offering clear, specific facts without hyperbole.

They're also not useful if they're not targeted and don't reach the right people. Releases need to serve as reference points for a pitch—not as the entirety of a pitch. Shotgun-style PR that blasts information to all corners of the media world simply doesn't work. Discourse can only be created by interested, relevant parties.

That requires relationships. I've always held a firm belief in the power of relationships, and I've been on both sides—as a journalist and as a PR professional. I've seen the landscape of media and PR communications shift dramatically over the years. The digital era, while offering a lot of benefits, has also led to a certain loss of human connection. It's like we're broadcasting messages off a cliff, with the listener at the bottom of the canyon. Sure, the message is heard, but the connection is lost somewhere along the way.

Think about the old days when a shopkeeper for a general store would know each customer personally. They knew about their lives, their families, their joys, and their sorrows. This connection, this bond, fostered a loyalty that allowed both the vendor and the customer to grow together. But in this age of digital communication, people are reduced to numbers in a spreadsheet. That bond, that connection, is being lost.

That same thing is happening with media connections. In the past, there were only a few outlets to think about—four major television networks, a local newspaper—that was about it. Now most people don't even have cable anymore, at least not exclusively. So, there are many, many more channels available to connect with audiences.

Don't get me wrong; I'm not dismissing the benefits of digital tools. They've opened up massive opportunities, especially in e-commerce, and have allowed companies to grow much faster. But they've also made it easier to send a mass email than to create a genuine connection with someone.

So, how do you rise above the noise? Be thoughtful. Understand both the person you're reaching out to and their audience. Ask them questions about themselves. Build a relationship, whether it's through a call, a Zoom meeting, or a coffee date if you live in the same city. You need to get to know these people and build a relationship. It becomes all too painfully apparent when you don't know who you're talking to or who their audience is.

Here's an extreme example of that and the massive backlash that resulted. There's an editor at *Outside Magazine* who's well known in the outdoor industry space because he has some very strong opinions and he's well respected. He got so energized about a pitch he received that he posted the pitch on his Instagram feed and just blasted the PR professional, who was from a major PR agency and representing a major brand. He called the publicist out and literally posted a screenshot of the pitch with nothing scrubbed for his massive number of followers to see. It was clearly a cut-and-paste pitch. The publicist spelled the writer's name wrong. He had the wrong name for the media outlet. This editor said, "This is not a serious person, so I'm going to delete him. I'm going to block him and then I'm going to call him out on social media."

Now that's brutal; I don't see that happen very often. But it really illustrates the importance of knowing your audience—in this case, an editor's beat and the very basic stuff like how to spell his name and the name of the outlet he writes for.

Building relationships is not a transactional process. If you're only paying influencers or buying ads, the coverage goes away when you stop writing checks. But if you take the time to understand the media landscape and get to know the people as well as you know your own customers, that's a much better long-term recipe for success.

While these traditional practices still have their place, and tools like press releases are still important, e-commerce and the rise in direct-to-consumer (D2C) interactions are changing these traditional practices. One major shift is that we now have far more opportunities to have direct conversations with consumers. We don't have to rely on the gatekeepers as much anymore. We can get our messages, unfiltered, to our audiences.

D2C AND DIRECT COMMUNICATIONS DEMAND A POSITIVE CX

As we've discussed, the rise of e-commerce has enabled brands to establish a direct-to-consumer (D2C) relationship, which has become an essential part of a company's communication program. This D2C relationship allows brands to communicate directly with the public, influencing the postsale experience significantly. The way a brand communicates with its customers can make a significant difference in their experience.

Whether it's media relations or public relations, the key is to communicate effectively and transparently with your audience. In a D2C relationship, this communication becomes even more critical, as it directly influences the customer's experience with the brand. If I go to Whole Foods and I want to buy something and they don't have the brand I want, I don't get grumpy because that's just life. You just go find the closest next best thing on the shelf, and you put it in your cart and go on with your life. But, if I'm going to order something direct, and they're going to charge me for it, they'd better deliver. If they don't, I'm not happy. There's a different expectation for the D2C relationship than there is with a retail store.

Most businesses, or brands, are going to mess up in big and small ways. That's not really what makes consumers mad or causes them to switch brands. It's more about how they respond when they mess up. When things go wrong with an organization, a product, messaging, or a campaign, they must be owned. They can't be ignored. They can't be swept under the rug or minimized through a clever PR campaign.

Now, fortunately, these kinds of big crises don't happen that often. But even in the absence of some major crisis, brands are at risk of somehow disappointing and, ultimately, losing their customers if they're not paying attention and engaging with them effectively. I'm sure we can all recount examples from our own interactions as consumers or customers. I know I can.

This lesson applies to any business, from a PR and marketing agency to a manufacturer, to museums, events, or retailers. Whether your company is B2B, B2C, or anything in between, every business exists to serve their customers' needs in a frictionless way. Friction at any point in the customer relationship is a risk. Your leadership team's mission should be to find the friction in delivering the customer what they paid for and eliminate it.

If you're a brand selling D2C, you need to deliver on your promises. The D2C model can offer improved margins, opportunities to develop brand loyalty, and increased control over brand packaging and reputation. But it also requires you to manage the whole purchase and delivery process, ensuring customer satisfaction. You have to be aware of and attentive to the entire funnel of a campaign. If you fail to engage and serve your customers appropriately, you risk losing them, just like Groundwork Coffee lost me.

Transparency and authenticity are key in building a brand that connects with its customers. Promptly addressing feedback, admitting mistakes, and providing solutions when issues arise shows a brand's dedication to customer satisfaction. Remember this: Your customers are not just a source of revenue. They're people who trust you to deliver on your promises. If you fail to engage and serve them appropriately, you risk losing them. And once a customer is lost, they're not easy to win back.

Chipotle's experience illustrates the power of radical transparency well.

They successfully rebounded from a crisis where their food made people sick, which is a worst-case scenario for any food service company. To address this, they used all their different media opportunities to communicate directly with their customers, admitting their mistake, explaining how they were going to fix it, and reassuring customers of their commitment to their brand standards and mission. This approach allowed them to regain their customers' trust and convince them to give the brand another chance. Eight years later, they're still here.

PR should be about communicating truth, not manipulating reality into a lie.

The audience, the organization, and the discourse between them are the perfect storm that has changed everything in the modern media landscape. That change is only going to accelerate as we make our way toward an even greater connection and an even faster discourse.

TAKEAWAYS

How prepared are you to deal with a crisis situation that has the potential to damage your brand?

→ Consider a situation where your company faces a crisis similar to Chipotle's. What steps could you take to address the issue and communicate with your key audiences to protect your brand?

→ How transparent are your communications? Review recent communications to determine how you could have been more open or honest and create a plan to increase transparency in the future.

→ What mechanisms do you have for customer feedback? How responsive are you to these channels? How do you act on this input and use it to improve?

→ Identify a competitor that has faced a PR crisis successfully. What lessons could you apply to your own PR and customer-engagement strategies?

→ When is your product/service most likely to be relevant to the larger news cycle? Do you have a plan for utilizing that moment?

CHAPTER 6

LEADING THE PACK:

We've talked before about MrBeast and his ability to grow and engage with very large audiences to establish his brand. His experience is especially relevant here as we talk about authority marketing in the digital era. MrBeast has been able to multipurpose his content to share it across various channels, achieving impact in very cost-effective and viral ways. He's used both earned and owned media as a force multiplier, extending the reach of his content very cost effectively.

In fact, MrBeast has become synonymous with viral content. And he's really cracked the code on repurposing content. He doesn't just create a video; he creates a content empire out of that video, spreading pieces of it across the globe in different languages and across different platforms. It's genius. His strategy isn't just about getting views—it's about grabbing attention from every corner of the internet in cost-effective ways to boost revenue. It's about multipurposing content in a way that transforms viewers into a loyal community of advocates.

So, how does he do this? Well, he has his own production company, which certainly helps, but he uses that production company very strategically. I've heard him talk in interviews about how he'll produce a piece of content, let's say a video, and promote that content on YouTube, which is his main channel. But he doesn't stop there. Next, he'll cut that content down to produce a mini version that he can share on Instagram and TikTok—and he'll cross-promote that content across these platforms, always driving traffic back to YouTube.

One of the things MrBeast discovered early on was the value of expanding his audience—in essence, his market—beyond English-speaking people. He figured out that the English-speaking audience represents a relatively small percentage of the global viewership on YouTube. So, he launched a voice dubbing company—Creator Global—to expand his reach. He's been experimenting with YouTube's multitrack audio since 2021—and he's offering the service to others. He first reached out to a Hispanic audience, hiring one of the most well-known actors in Mexico to dub all his videos. So, it's the exact same video, but it's dubbed in Spanish using a widely recognized voice. Viewers engage with the content because they're already comfortable with the voice. Then he created a Portuguese channel. Then Japanese. Then Chinese. The video is already created; all he's doing is extending its reach through the use of recognizable talent in other geographies.

It's likely that his thought process went something like this: I have this video content in English. If I dub it over in five other languages for a fraction of the cost it took me to make the video in the first place, I can deploy it on all these other channels to target new audiences.

I get all this extra attention and extra revenue basically for the same money I already spent. Then I'm going to promote it.

INFLUENCERS, THOUGHT LEADERS, AND AFFILIATES

Under the umbrella of authority marketing are three important concepts: thought leaders, influencers, and affiliates.

Thought Leaders

Thought leadership is about using content to influence thinking and create conversations around a topic that an individual or brand is considered an expert in. It's about the value of the information provided and its positive impact on an audience. Thought leaders are people or brands that others turn to as trusted advisors or sources of important and credible information. The goal is to develop credibility among a specific target audience, often to promote and sell products and services and to establish the thought leader as a go-to source for insights and solutions. Thought leaders tend to have some innate authority or expertise in a particular field.

Malcolm Gladwell is an author known for books including *Outliers, Tipping Point,* and *Blink*. The thread that runs through all his books, blog posts, and articles is that he takes a long, hard look at different aspects of people who have accomplished impressive things in life, business, and leadership and asks "why" over and over, digging down to understand not just how they accomplished something— but why they attempted it in the first place and what allowed them to achieve results where others could not. The books are successful, which gave Gladwell the platform to then give talks and seminars about the very nature of success.

From there he started appearing on podcasts discussing the topic, then started his own podcast called *Revisionist History*. The show was successful, so he then built a production company around it called Pushkin Industries that produced other similar shows. Gladwell now runs a multifaceted media machine that turns out content (his and others') in a variety of formats for a variety of platforms, all based on the concept of figuring out how people succeed. And people are willing to pay for that content in all its forms because he's established himself as an expert in this specific area. That is thought leadership.

Influencers

Influencers also have a goal of generating awareness and building an audience that may be used to sell products and services—or views. But, unlike thought leaders, influencers don't necessarily have any innate authority or expertise aside from their ability to build an audience. MrBeast, whom we've talked about, is an influencer who has built a substantial audience that generates significant revenue based on his ability to create and distribute content online in ways that his audience finds interesting.

Another example of this is my friend Larry Chen. I first met Larry when he was a young motorsports photographer shooting for a car culture website called SpeedHunters. Larry was *very* good and eager to shoot new things, so we started hiring him as a freelancer for a variety of different events and programs. Larry is also incredibly enthusiastic about both cars and photography, and his kind, friendly, and outgoing nature radiates out of him in every conversation. That combination of talent and personality has served him well, and it has been exciting to watch his career grow over the years. At first, he stayed behind the camera, and his notoriety came from his photos published in an ever-increasing lineup of media sites and magazines. Then he started appearing in content on the popular Hoonigan YouTube channel, and eventually he started his own channel that took off.

Because Larry is talented, but also authentic and relatable, people are drawn to him. The channel took off, which allowed him to book more shoots and grow his business from a single shooter to a team of creators that travel the world documenting car culture of all kinds. It also put him on the radar of some very big companies, and Larry is now an official Canon "Ambassador of Light" running seminars and workshops for the camera company, and he's sponsored by Toyota, which works with him on custom car builds.

For all these reasons, we worked with the Specialty Equipment Market Association (SEMA)—the main trade association and trade show for the automotive industry—to name Larry its first Content Creator of the Year. He is an influencer in the truest sense of the word—his content, personality, and perspective *influence* people to try new things.

Through their social media presence and content creation, influencers review products, share experiences, and influence their followers' purchasing decisions. In fact, their influence has proven to be so significant in the digital environment that the Federal Trade Commission (FTC) has established rules requiring them to make it readily apparent when they are posting or sharing information about a product or service that they have some material relationship with—in other words, they make money based on the clicks, shares, and sales they generate.

Affiliates

Influencers are not always compensated for their ability to generate interest in a product or service. When they are, they could also be viewed as affiliates. Affiliate marketing is an extension of influence—a mutually beneficial partnership where content creators and brands collaborate to drive sales.

With affiliate marketing, someone with something to sell teams up with someone who has a relevant online audience that aligns with their potential customer base. For every lead or sale generated, the affiliate receives payment—in cash, equity, or both. Podcasters and people or brands with websites are two primary examples of how affiliate marketing works. Joe Rogan is one notable example. On his podcast, *The Joe Rogan Experience,*[17] he talks about supplements like Athletic Greens and Alpha Brain—because in lieu of traditional "pay to play" advertising, he has an affiliate deal with the companies that gives him a "piece of the action." I don't know the terms of his deals with these companies, but he has openly stated he has an ownership stake, thereby incentivizing him to talk about the products to his very sizeable audience. But—and this is an important but—he also truly believes in the products, and they're aligned with his brand. Affiliate marketing is about creating win-win partnerships where everyone— the brand, the affiliate, and the customer—benefits.

Together, thought leadership, influencer, and affiliate marketing are part of a broader approach known as authority marketing—the use of recognition, expertise, and an audience to establish brand credibility and, subsequently, sales.

It's a twenty-first-century style of earned media.

INFLUENCE THROUGH STRATEGIC CONTENT GENERATION

MrBeast is an example of an influencer with a massive audience of followers who not only consume his content but also follow his rec-

---

17   "The Joe Rogan Experience," *Joe Rogan,* June 14, 2024, https://www.joerogan.com/.

ommendations. He has influence with them. Influence can be closely tied to thought leadership. In fact, the two can work hand in hand. MrBeast's engagement with a well-known thought leader—Elon Musk—illustrates this.

MrBeast's influence stems from his ability to grow a massive audience. Elon Musk also has a massive audience, but he is a thought leader based on his reputation and expertise in the business world.

When Musk came across MrBeast's videos on YouTube, he was intrigued. He suggested that MrBeast consider X's (formerly Twitter's) video platform, and he did it publicly on the channel. This set the stage for an experiment that would take place in full view of both of their massive audiences. MrBeast released a video of a comparison between a one-dollar car and one purportedly worth $100 million.[18] It quickly gained significant attention, likely due to the anticipation that had been built through the very public interaction between the two men. This, coupled with the placement of a few ads around the content, led to a revenue share of $250,000 in just a few days.[19]

This kind of reach isn't just available to the big brands or the major influencers. Another real-world example comes from my own family, my dad, who owned an HVAC company in a suburb of Los Angeles.

When my dad sold his HVAC business, the new owners quickly sought visibility with both his existing customers and potential new

---

18 "MrBeast's $1 Car vs. $100,000,000 Car Video on Elon Musk's X Has Received Over 100M Views: Is It a Success?" *Benzinga*, June 14, 2024, https://www.benzinga.com/news/24/01/36690091/mrbeasts-1-car-vs-100-000-000-car-video-on-elon-musks-x-has-received-over-100m-views-is-it-a-success.

19 V. Tomar, "MrBeast Planning to Take Over Twitter? Fans Revisit the YouTuber's Hilarious Conversation with Elon Musk," EssentiallySports, July 4, 2023, https://www.essentiallysports.com/esports-news-mrbeast-planning-to-take-over-twitter-fans-revisit-the-youtubers-hilarious-conversation-with-elon-musk/.

customers based on a very local geography. They went to their service department and said: "Every time you get a five-star review on Google, we're going to give you $100. If you get five in a week, you'll not only get $500, but we'll give you an additional $500." That was potentially up to $1,000 extra in a week just for basically doing their jobs, so a strong incentive to generate reviews.

The process of generating reviews was pretty straightforward. Service people just had to ask for the review. "How was my service? Did you have a good experience? If you did, please leave me a five-star review. I really appreciate it." You've likely received the same type of requests from businesses you frequent. Along with the ask was a CRM that could automate the process of following up with customers. After the customer paid for service, they got a prompt reminding them to leave a review.

But the new owners didn't stop there. They further leveraged the value of these five-star reviews, using them as a force multiplier. As reviews started to come in, which they did immediately, they screen captured the reviews in real time and posted them across all their social channels. This is what we call "social proof," meaning that instead of creating posts for social media telling potential customers "We're the best," the company was showing people other actual customer reviews that raved about their service. It feels much more authentic and has a much bigger impact.

That's not all that different from what MrBeast has done in terms of strategically using content across multiple channels to build audience and generate awareness and engagement. It's just the local small business version of using content strategically—or content marketing. Doing this allows brands to leverage their existing audience while building a new audience as content is liked and shared—in some cases "going viral."

THE ROLE OF AUTHORITY MARKETING IN MODERN PR

Authority marketing is a broad term that can encompass the impacts of influencers, thought leaders, and affiliates.

As we've seen, both thought leadership and authority marketing have been around for decades and have been leveraged by marketers and brands to raise awareness, build audiences, and drive sales.

They're similar concepts that can work in tandem.

Authority marketing isn't overtly about selling a product or service; it's about offering value through the unique knowledge and insights that you can provide. When you share your expertise, you're building trust and credibility with your audience.

We've seen how some of the very early marketing influencers like Edward Bernays and Samuel Zemurray were able to successfully leverage the power of PR—and yes, PR stunts—way back in the early twentieth century. And we've seen how more modern era thought leaders like MrBeast continue to use PR stunts to capture attention and earn influence. But, PR stunts aren't just about creating buzz; they're about making a statement that resonates with your audience—that moves and influences them.

That's what Bernays did when he turned smoking cigarettes into a chic act of civil disobedience. And that's not too much different than getting an influencer to demo your product on TikTok today. It's about creating disruption and getting people to talk about your product in a way that feels organic and true to your brand.

Perhaps one of the big differences in terms of opportunity today is that thought leadership isn't just for the few and the mighty. It's for anyone with a message and the ability to build an audience.

Through D2C marketing, individuals and brands of all sizes have the ability to get their messages in front of audiences literally around the globe. Historically, this was done through the use of earned media—getting others, generally reporters and media representatives, to share information about your products. Earned media still plays a role today, but it can now be augmented through D2C outreach and owned media—the channels you have available to you to share information like your website, a blog, or videos on YouTube.

Building an audience requires authenticity, but it also requires capturing the attention of that audience. That's something that can be done through PR stunts—the kind that historical pros (like Bernays and Zemurray) and modern-day PR pros (like MrBeast) have successfully used.

SNOOP DOGG AND AUTHORITY MARKETING

Snoop Dogg is another example of the impact of authority marketing and the role that PR stunts still play in capturing attention and building audience.

Snoop Dogg is quite widely known not only for his entertainment talent but also for his association with smoking—specifically smoking marijuana. Since he first appeared on Dr. Dre's pivotal album *The Chronic* in 1992, Snoop has been a very public marijuana advocate. More than thirty years, 35 million albums sold, seventeen Grammy nominations, an Emmy Award, and hundreds of TV and film appearances later, Snoop is an American cultural icon. He has also continued to be a very public advocate for pot. In 2015 alone, he backed or founded several marijuana-based businesses, including Eaze, one of the first marijuana delivery services in California; Merry Jane, a marijuana news and digital media outlet; and his own line of actual cannabis products, Leafs by Snoop.

It's fair with that type of résumé to say Snoop is a marijuana authority, and one of particularly high visibility. When a fire pit company, Solo Stove, decided to capitalize on Snoop Dogg's image and authority by enlisting his participation in a campaign that was initially shared on his Instagram and X accounts, he shockingly declared that after "much consideration and conversation," he had decided to "give up smoke."[20]

That proclamation immediately sparked interest and the kind of buzz the brand intended. People were intrigued by the idea that one of the world's most famous advocates for marijuana had given up the habit. Social posts went wild and racked up massive reach and engagement, driving coverage by the traditional media both online and even on cable news and TV. It was real breaking news. After the initial pop of coverage, it was revealed that the real story behind the messages was quite different than perceived and that he was simply plugging the smokeless fire pit.

It was, in essence, a stunt.

Whether it was a stunt that resulted, or will result, in a sales boost is unclear. As an interesting aside, at the time this book was written in mid-2024, the CEO of Solo Stove has resigned, and the company has announced it's going in a new direction. So, does that mean the campaign was a success, or a failure? It certainly drove massive awareness and earned media around the Solo Stove brand and name, and while I don't have access to the back end of their website stats, I'm willing to bet their site traffic skyrocketed for a time. So, they got what they wanted from Snoop. Did they do everything they could to capture and convert that awareness to sales? Do they have the D2C

---

20   G. Vivinetto, "Snoop Dogg Clears Up Post Stating He 'Decided to Give Up Smoke,'" *Today*, November 20, 2023, https://www.today.com/popculture/news/snoop-dogg-giving-up-smoke-meaning-rcna126021.

systems or distribution to take advantage of it? We don't know the answer to that question yet. What it does illustrate, though, is how public forums can be used to get people talking about a product by capturing interest and intention and driving public dialogue.

PR stunts are strategic actions designed to create disruption in the news cycle, generating public interest and conversation. The goal of a PR stunt is to insert a brand's message into the public dialogue in an organic way that sparks discussion. As the Snoop Dogg example illustrates, celebrities can be leveraged in PR stunts to reach a broader audience and gain immediate interest.

It's important to note, though, that it's not only the immediate impact of a PR stunt that should be used to determine its effectiveness but also its sustained impact and alignment with broader marketing goals. To be most effective, PR stunts should be part of a comprehensive marketing strategy that includes earned, owned, and paid media, as well as D2C messaging. The goal is to impact consumer behavior by using consumer psychology to drive attention, interest, conversation, and ultimately a sale that leads to loyalty and advocacy.

INFLUENCERS AND AFFILIATES IN MODERN PR

Influencers and affiliates are two important players in today's PR and media landscape. They represent individuals and organizations that brands can leverage to expand their audiences and extend their messages.

Snoop Dogg is an example of an influencer—someone who has authority, name recognition, and the power to influence an audience. Influencers today are a critical component of modern PR and marketing. Snoop Dogg is a celebrity influencer already known for his talent as a rapper and songwriter. Other influencers emerge more organically—like MrBeast, who we've already discussed, along with similar influencers like Zach King, PewDiePie, Khabane "Khaby" Lame, Larry Chen, and Daniel Mac, who have been identified as top Instagram influencers who are noncelebrities.[21]

Influencers play an important role in today's PR and marketing efforts for most brands. Another role that has become very important to raise awareness and generate sales is affiliates.

AFFILIATE MARKETING AND ITS HISTORICAL CONTEXT

Affiliates are people or companies that brands partner with to bring their messages to new audiences or to reinforce their messages. Affiliates generally receive payment for their efforts, often some percentage of leads or sales generated. The success of their efforts is generally tracked through links or codes that can tie leads and sales back to their efforts.

Affiliate marketing isn't really anything new. It's actually a digital form of commission-based sales. While affiliate marketing has become increasingly prevalent since the 1990s and the advent of the digital marketing environment, its history actually extends back to earlier decades. Consider, for instance, the business model of companies like Avon, Tupperware, and Amway, which leveraged the networks of consumers to sell products to their friends and relatives in exchange for compensation and products.

But affiliate marketing has exploded in an environment where digital commerce is rampant and widely used. It offers an extension of an influencer through a content creator model where authenticity is the name of the game. By partnering with affiliates who align with your brand's values, you're not just reaching more people; you're building a community of advocates who believe in what you're doing.

---

21   Team Klug, "Top Instagram Influencers Non-celebrity," KlugKlug, October 31, 2023, https://klugklug.com/top-instagram-influencers-non-celebrity/.

It's a powerful way to expand your reach and deepen the connections you make.

One of the earliest examples of affiliate marketing was Amazon's Associates program, which was launched in 1996. It allowed websites to link to Amazon products and earn a commission on any sales generated through those links.

The moral of the story here is that affiliate marketing isn't—or shouldn't be—just about making a quick buck. Like any other successful form of PR, it's about building genuine and authentic relationships. Rogan's approach to affiliate marketing is really a master class for anyone thinking about making their own mark in the affiliate space.

SOCIAL MEDIA AND USING CONTENT TO FUEL YOUR AUTHORITY MARKETING

Content plays a major role in getting brand messages out to audiences of all kinds—and not just a single form of content. People interact with content in different ways and have varying preferences for how they consume information. Brands need to meet them where they are. They also need to influence them. That can best be done when the producer of that content, or the name behind the content, is recognized and trusted. Building trust, as we've discussed, is based on authenticity and aligning messaging with brand attributes consistently over time. It's a strategic endeavor that should be designed to link brand messages to audience needs and interests.

Social media has become a game changer for marketers in the digital environment. It's revolutionized how brands connect with audiences and has provided unprecedented opportunities for engagement, storytelling, and brand building. Whether it's through compelling content, strategic collaborations, or interactive campaigns, social media is where your brand comes to life. It's where you can tell your story and engage with your audience in real time.

Leveraging the power of social media in brand building isn't just for the big brands. Social media has really democratized the ability to get messages in front of audiences of all types and sizes.

Authority marketing—which from a content leadership standpoint we can call "you-driven marketing"—benefits significantly from today's digital marketing channels and social media. As we've seen, just about anybody can become an authority on anything by identifying and understanding an audience, finding places where there's synergy between their values and what their audience values, and delivering content in authentic and valuable ways. If you want to be known as the go-to person in your field, whatever that field is, you need to have a plan, and you need to create and share content regularly.

So, for instance, let's say you're using LinkedIn to connect with a B2B audience. There's a whole strategy behind how to do this. It might look something like this:

First, commit to commenting on at least three high-visibility posts a day. If you can reshare at least one high-visibility post a day and create your own high-visibility posts at least once a day, every day, for five days a week, for a year, in most cases, you're going to have five or ten times the following you initially had on LinkedIn. This strategy can be especially powerful if you're focused on a specific niche.

You might also go in and follow all the thought leaders in your field on LinkedIn. These are people who are reaching the same audience you want to reach, but they've already gained traction. They already have an audience. They already know the kind of content that appeals to that audience. So, every time they have a breakout post that goes viral, save it. Over time, you'll amass a significant archive of saved posts. Then go back to the beginning of those posts and let them inspire you to create your own posts on the same subject matter.

LinkedIn's algorithms know which posts have a higher probability of going viral than others because they know which content has already performed well on the platform. Understanding which content resonates with your audience—by paying close attention to what established thought leaders are doing—can help you create targeted content designed to get traction.

Now, note that I'm not suggesting that you simply copy and paste what others are doing. I'm suggesting that you just become inspired by that content and then come up with your own take on the same subject matter. Becoming a thought leader isn't about being just like someone else; it's about being uniquely you. That's an example of a simple growth hack that you can do on LinkedIn. And it's the same approach that also works on other social media platforms. Where you decide to establish your authority depends on your audience, your brand, and your goals.

Another tool that really works well on LinkedIn, and other channels, is video. A great example of a thought leader who really leveraged this is Erica Ayers Badan, who was the CEO of Barstool Sports after Dave Portnoy. Ultimately, she handed the reins back to Portnoy, but while she was in that role, she was a very strong leader with a really engaging personality. She used that personality effectively in establishing herself as an authority with LinkedIn as her primary platform.

On an almost daily basis, she did what she called "one-to-ones," which might feature her in a cab or an Uber going to a meeting, or sitting in her sweats at the gym, or working at her desk. People would submit questions that might be about Barstool or just about leadership. And she'd answer people's questions in a very raw and candid way. It was authentic, and it was on video and posted almost every day. So, they were timely and compelling.

Video works very well, even on LinkedIn, as Badan's example illustrates. The algorithm really likes video. According to LinkedIn's own data, video posts on the channel generate five times more engagement compared to other types of content like text or image posts.[22]

Public speaking can be another great way to establish yourself as an authority. Start small by offering to speak at trade conferences or for small gatherings of business leaders. Shoot video of your presentations so you can post that in digital channels and use it to get bigger speaking gigs. Try to get yourself into a TEDx talk. Try to get yourself into a major trade conference. Capture your content, share it across social channels, and turn it into teaser videos. As we've seen through MrBeast's examples, multipurposing your content is a great way to extend your reach without extending the amount of time you have to invest in doing so.

You can take video of your presentations, put it up on your website, post a link to it in a blog post or social media posts, and cut it down into a three-second clip along with a listicle that you can post on LinkedIn, Facebook, or other channels. Expand your coverage through a podcast that you can use to talk about the subject matter that you're an expert on and bring in guests who can not only add to your narrative but also help to promote the content through their own channels. Just reach out to experts in your field and say, "Hey, come on my podcast and talk about yourself." Even if your podcast is small, most people will say yes.

All these things are part of a thought leadership ecosystem where you're using authority marketing to build awareness and, ultimately,

22   "LinkedIn Video Marketing Statistics," *Here/Now,* June 14, 2024, https://www.herenow.
film/trimtab/linkedin-video-marketing-statistics.

to grow your company and your product or service line. It's all about differentiation, reach, and the strategic and consistent sharing of content that your audience is interested in.

TAKEAWAYS

Direct-to-consumer engagement is important in our digital marketing environment, as we've seen. As part of this engagement, though, brands have an opportunity to engage with affiliate marketers and influencers to expand and support their messaging.

➔ **PR stunts** are nothing new, but a digital environment makes them more accessible to almost anyone. How could you create buzz through a PR stunt that is relevant to both your brand and your audience's interest in the same manner as Edward Bernays and MrBeast have done?

➔ **Anyone with a message and the ability to build an audience can become a thought leader.** How could you share your expertise to build trust and credibility?

➔ **Capitalize on your owned media**—your website, social channels, blog, podcast, etc.—to share information and build or extend your audience. What unique, compelling, and valuable information do you have to provide to your audience?

➔ **How could you repurpose your content across multiple channels?**

➔ **Who are the influencers and affiliates** in your area of expertise with an audience you could leverage to extend your own brand's reach? How could you engage with them to help spread your message to a larger audience?

CHAPTER 7

CROSSING THE FINISH LINE:

The journey from strategy to success in PR is often filled with unexpected twists and turns, as this story will illustrate. What it also illustrates is that, although we talk about metrics, key performance indicators (KPIs), and all kinds of objective measurable stuff, some of the real "aha!" moments don't necessarily come from the numbers but from real-world observations.

A few years ago, we were approached by a well-known luxury aftermarket wheel company. This was a very well-regarded brand that sells a hand-finished product that's priced more in line with fine jewelry than car parts. They specialized in high-end, custom wheels, forged and machined in America—a rarity even today. With prices ranging from $10,000 to $20,000 for a set of wheels, their products are truly the epitome of luxury and were designed for the most exquisite hypercars and sports cars.

The company had already made a name for itself in the enthusiast space due to the work of a competent marketer who had secured some solid PR and social media traction. But they were hoping to shift gears. The goal? To transcend the aftermarket auto parts label and be recognized as a bona fide luxury goods brand on a global scale.

Our strategy was multifaceted. We elevated their social media content, collaborated with influencers, and made a bold move to cease all advertising in automotive media. Instead, we targeted high-end lifestyle outlets, using the term *bespoke* to describe their wheels—custom tailored to each owner's unique preferences. Our efforts paid off, landing stories in prestigious publications like the *Robb Report* and even snagging the cover of the *Amex Black Card* magazine.

But the most interesting part of our journey began when we noticed something unusual in our back-end data. Despite the majority of the brand's sales being domestic, there was a significant spike in social media engagement from Riyadh, Saudi Arabia. While the company did have strong international sales, their numbers in Saudi Arabia were almost zero, despite a seemingly high level of interest in its content there. This piqued our curiosity. Why Riyadh? Most importantly, why wasn't this engagement translating into sales?

Because we were intrigued, we decided to delve deeper. Our investigation led us to Riyadh's most luxurious dealership, which boasted a stunning display of our client's wheels. The setup was perfect, but the sales were virtually nonexistent.

Why? A cultural oversight. What we learned was that our client's logo—a shield with a Swiss cross—was inadvertently offending potential buyers in this devout Muslim country where displaying a cross in public is against the law. This insight led us to suggest an alternative logo, without the cross, for the center caps of the wheels. It was a minor tweak that had a major impact. Sales in Riyadh skyrocketed, transforming it into one of our client's most lucrative markets.

This experience taught us a very valuable lesson about the importance of aligning KPIs with business goals. It's not just about monitoring social engagement or increasing brand visibility. It's about understanding the nuances of your target market, asking the right questions, and being willing to adapt your strategy to meet your unique goals.

As Simon Sinek has famously said: "Start with why."[23] In our case, persistently asking "why" led us to a simple yet transformative solution. It's a great example to illustrate the power of aligning every action, every strategy, and every KPI with the business goals you're trying to achieve. It's also a testament to the power that people still bring to the table no matter how sophisticated the data or the technology used to crunch the data. Human insights still make a difference.

In PR and marketing, the bottom line is results. Sure, PR can be a lot of fun, and I won't deny it. It's a creative field, and its potential for creativity has increased dramatically since the emergence of a wide range of digital channels that allow brands and business owners to own their own media and reach out directly to a wide range of audiences.

But effective PR isn't only about being creative to get attention, win awards, or just have fun. It's about achieving results. Without results, there's really no purpose or meaning behind any of your PR efforts, no matter how clever they are—or how viral they may become.

---

23 Simon Sinek, *Start with Why: How Great Leaders Inspire Everyone to Take Action* (Portfolio, 2009).

MOVING AWAY FROM "PR BY THE POUND"

Effective PR is about setting goals, measuring impact, and sticking to a plan. A lot has changed in terms of how we do this from the "old days" of PR. Back in the day, measuring the success of PR campaigns was like trying to catch smoke with your bare hands. We relied heavily on print media, and while getting a story in a major publication felt like a win, quantifying its impact was a different story. It was all about "PR by the pound," where more coverage supposedly meant better performance. Measuring the performance of a campaign was less about awareness and conversion to sales and more about trying to justify your existence and budget. In fact, a former boss at a prior agency used to determine the success of a campaign with what he called "thud factor," which meant at the end of the campaign he'd have us print out all the media hits, have them spiral bound, and then drop the book on his desk. If it made a thud, that was a winner. If it didn't … you had a tough conversation at the office. But honestly, it was more of a guessing game than anything else.

Now, fast-forward to today, and it's a whole new ball game. Tools like Looker Studio, Semrush, Critical Mention, and HubSpot have changed everything. We can track real-time data, see where our audiences are coming from, and measure engagement down to the click. It's no longer about guessing—it's about knowing.

Looker Studio has been a game changer. It allows us to see exactly how our campaigns are performing across different platforms. We can track website traffic, monitor social media engagement, and even keep an eye on paid ad performance. It's about having the full picture and being able to adjust on the fly to get the best results. Sometimes an entire campaign that drives earned media coverage across dozens of sites doesn't move the needle even a bit. Other times a single story in the right outlet can cause a sales explosion. Not every hit does what you expect, which is why it's so important to clarify your wins and KPIs *before* the campaign starts and then track the results—so you can learn. Learn about your audience, what drives interest and awareness, and what moves the needle in terms of performance and sales.

This shift to data-driven PR isn't just about proving ROI, though; it's about constantly refining our strategies to make sure we're hitting the mark. Being able to show clients concrete data that backs up our efforts is pretty satisfying.

But the real-time feedback and tracking capabilities we have now don't just benefit us as PR pros; they empower our clients too. Our clients can see the direct impact of their PR investments, which builds trust and drives future strategies.

The immediacy of digital marketing and analytics, though, can also lead to unreasonable expectations. Achieving measurable results through PR and marketing takes time.

A MARATHON, NOT A SPRINT

Clients, business owners, and brand managers can be impatient when it comes to seeing results from their PR and marketing efforts. The digital environment is so immediate that some think that success is simply a matter of posting something or sharing a video and sitting back to rack up the revenue.

That's not the case, of course. PR and marketing aren't just a switch you flip on for instant sales. It can take months to really gain traction and see results from your PR efforts, whether they're earned, owned, or paid. Too often, brands give up before they've really given their efforts a chance to pay off. That can be the result of failing to plan in the first place. I've seen too many companies bail at the first sign of trouble, but that's not how this works. It's about A/B testing, brand impressions, and content that resonates.

And it's about having a plan. You've probably heard the old saying "If you fail to plan, you're planning to fail." That's definitely true in the new world of PR; it has to start with a plan.

STRATEGIC PLANNING IN PR

Imagine you're setting out on a cross-country road trip. You wouldn't just jump in the car and drive, right? You'd plan your route, check your car, and make sure you know where you're going. You'd probably have a destination in mind, a budget, and a timeframe for when you'd like to reach your destination. You'd plan out pitstops along the way—places to grab a bite to eat or spend a night.

That's what strategic planning in PR is all about. It's about understanding where you want your brand to go and mapping out how to get there. It's not just about putting out a message—it's about putting out the right message, in the right places, at the right times. There are several steps involved in this process.

First, you need to conduct a situational analysis. You need to know where you stand before you can plan where you're going. This means taking a hard look at your current PR and marketing efforts, understanding your market position, and identifying your strengths and weaknesses. You need to understand your position in the market, especially related to your competitors. You've got to have a value proposition that shines and a brand manifesto that tells the world who you are. Think Patagonia: they know who they are, and they're not afraid to show it.

As we've already discussed, strategic planning is also going to involve defining your target audience very clearly and specifically— who are you trying to reach? What's important to them? What is it about your company and its products and services that is likely to hold value for them? Clearly understanding your audience is crucial to tailoring your messages and tactics.

You're then going to pick your channels of communication—some combination of earned, owned, and paid media. As we've seen, these days you have a wide range of options. You can't be everywhere—and you shouldn't be—so you need to decide which channels and which strategies are likely to be most effective for you.

Finally, you're going to consider what success—for you—looks like. You'll want to set clear and achievable goals. That might be increasing brand awareness by 20 percent or generating 30 percent more leads or boosting sales by 15 percent. Your objectives should be specific and measurable.

ALIGNING KPIS WITH BUSINESS GOALS

Your KPIs need to be aligned with your business goals. KPIs—or key performance indicators—are the metrics you'll use to determine the success of your PR and marketing efforts. They should directly relate to your business goals, be supportive of your brand, and provide insight into how well your strategies are performing. This could include metrics like brand awareness, lead generation, conversion rates, or customer retention.

Your KPIs will help you track progress, make informed decisions, and pivot when necessary. KPIs aren't just about sales—they're about brand awareness, engagement, and all the steps that lead to a final purchase. And, in fact, as we've seen, with the new marketing funnel your KPIs need to go even further to encompass loyalty and advocacy.

Once you've established your KPIs, you can identify the specific metrics that matter most for you. For example, if brand awareness is your goal, you might track media mentions or social media reach. If it's website traffic, you would look at website visits, click-through rates, and session durations.

Your KPIs are your KPIs. This isn't about just referring to a list of KPIs in some textbook or that some other brand manager uses. It's about considering your products and services, your brand, your audience, and your unique goals and strategies.

It's also not just about collecting data. It's about analyzing that data to make informed decisions that will drive your future PR and marketing efforts. This is where tools like analytics platforms, customer surveys, and media monitoring can come into play. They help you understand the impact of your efforts so you can adjust your strategies as needed.

Keep in mind that the world of PR and marketing is always evolving. What worked yesterday might not work tomorrow. You need to stay agile, keep testing, and never stop learning. By aligning your KPIs with your business goals and continuously optimizing your strategies, you'll not only reach your destination—you'll set new records.

SEO, ATTRIBUTION, AND THE "WIRE"

I think it's important to talk about how search, or search engine optimization (SEO), fits into the measurement picture. The big takeaway: it's just as important, if not more important, as it ever was. Google is still the big elephant in the room, and Google is all about search. In fact, 63.4 percent of all traffic referrals come from Google.[24]

People get confused and think that their social strategy is going to be good for search. It's not. It has nothing to do with search. Social platforms are walled gardens. Those that control these platforms want you to live there—and they want you to stay there. They don't want you to leave. In fact, their algorithms are specifically designed to keep you there. You can see this for yourself if you take a look at channels like LinkedIn or Facebook—or, especially, Instagram—that make it hard, if not impossible, to include links within your posts. So, you'll see people doing things like putting the link in a comment as a workaround. But it's a workaround that doesn't really work because the fact is that social media activity doesn't drive website traffic.

If you put a link into a post that goes to a site that's outside of that channel's ecosystem, it will kill your engagement. If, though, you upload a video, engagement will usually be very good. These channels want more people adding content into the scroll and the feed—content that will stay there. They don't want people pushing traffic outside of their walled gardens.

Now this may all change. TikTok might take over. Or TikTok might get banned. Who knows? In the meantime, though, Google is still by far the most dominant player. And that's not going to go away overnight. So, if that's the case, we have to be cognizant of that. That means that you have to make sure that your website is optimized for SEO. Do you have meta tags on all your posts and all your images? Are your images ADA compliant—adhering to the Americans with

24   R. Fishkin, "Who Sends Traffic on the Web and How Much? New Research from Datos & SparkToro," SparkToro, March 12, 2024, https://sparktoro.com/blog/who-sends-traffic-on-the-web-and-how-much-new-research-from-datos-sparktoro/.

Disabilities Act (ADA) Standards for Accessible Design? Is there video embedded into the site? Is it keyword-rich copy?

These are all important things. Of course, there's been a lot of predictions about how AI is going to upend this whole deal. But we're going to just have to wait and see on that one.

So, the important technical element of SEO is a very specific sort of engineering process. But the even more important element of SEO is high authority ranking. What that means is, are there other sites on the internet that are linking to your site? And, are they high authority ranking? Are they respected? Are they relevant? This is another reason that PR continues to be important in the future—earned media is a great way to get those links, whether it's *Newsweek* or you make some sort of technology hardware and it's TechCrunch or Gizmodo or Engadget. In fact, even if it's a small enthusiast forum that has really dedicated users, if they're linking to your site, that's going to help with search and site traffic—it's going to help Google find your site and put it on the first page.

That's a critical part of PR. And it's going to be one aspect of the KPIs you'll monitor to determine whether your efforts are generating the results you want. It's a different kind of PR, though, using different tools.

We often have clients coming to us wanting to put a new release out on the "wire." The wire is a newswire or service that distributes press releases to a network of media outlets, journalists, and online services. Historically, these services were a primary tool for PR pros to distribute their news and announcements to a broad audience quickly and efficiently. But in the era of digital marketing and SEO, the effectiveness of these wire services has declined for a number of reasons:

- **Nofollow links**: Most wire services use "nofollow" attributes on links in their press releases. These tell search engines not to pass on any link equity or ranking benefits to the linked pages. The reason for the change is primarily because Google's algorithm updates were attempting to reduce the impact of artificial link-building practices.

- **Spammy content**: Wire services made distributing press releases so easy that it wasn't long before there was an influx of very low-quality, spammy content. Companies started issuing releases for non-newsworthy events, diluting the value of the service—and reducing trust among journalists and readers.

- **Journalist preferences**: Journalists just don't rely on formal releases—and, especially, wire releases—anymore. They're more selective about the sources they use, and they generally prefer direct pitches and original content.

- **Cost/benefit**: Wire service distribution can be expensive and the return on investment often hard to justify.

In my opinion, the wire is almost useless at this point unless you're a publicly traded company and need to follow some SEC compliance rules for disclosure. The wire is a great compliance tool for that. But to spend $800 plus on the distribution of a release through a wire service to blast a release out that basically just gets pushed through RSS feeds really doesn't make sense in this new PR environment.

That's really where measurement comes into play. Using measurement tools can help you understand which of your efforts are working, which aren't, and where improvements could help boost results.

MEASUREMENT TOOLS

Another way that the world of PR and marketing has changed significantly over the past several years is our ability to measure and monitor our PR efforts in an objective way to help determine what works, what doesn't, and how we can most effectively adjust our efforts to achieve better results.

Looker Studio is an example of a tool we've discussed. It's revolutionized the way we can measure the effectiveness of our communication efforts. In the world of public relations, the ability to validate our work with concrete data has been a game changer. With Looker Studio, we can monitor a myriad of metrics that are crucial for understanding the impact of our clients' campaigns.

For instance, we can track inbound traffic to see how many people are visiting a client's website because of our PR efforts. We can monitor search trends to understand how our campaigns are influencing what people are looking for online. Organic social media performance is another key metric that gives us insight into how our content is resonating with audiences on platforms like Facebook and X (formerly Twitter) without paid promotion.

Paid social campaigns can also be monitored with Looker Studio. We can see how our paid ads are performing across social media platforms, ensuring that our clients' investments are yielding the desired results. We can track all the paid funnels, allowing us to see the customer journey from initial awareness through conversion.

Traffic referrals are another key metric we can monitor. Knowing where traffic is coming from helps us understand which publications and influencers are most effective at driving audiences to our clients' content. This is the kind of information that's really invaluable when it comes to refining our strategies and focusing our efforts where we know they'll have the most impact.

The beauty of Looker Studio is that it provides a clear view of what's working and what's not—in real time. This immediacy allows us to have informed conversations with clients about the effectiveness of their PR campaigns. We can show them tangible spikes in traffic following a successful media hit, which not only proves the value of PR but also helps guide future strategies. With Looker Studio, we have a way to measure the impact of our work like never before, making PR a more data-driven and accountable field.

Recently, though, we've expanded on the power of Looker Studio to offer another service to clients—or potential clients. The Accelerator program.

ACCELERATOR PROGRAM

There's another service that we offer that we call our Accelerator program. It's an opportunity for brands to work with us to analyze and evaluate their market positions with fresh eyes and expertise. For a one-time fee, we provide a thorough brand audit of all marketing channels to identify strengths, weaknesses, and areas of opportunity and improvement. We can determine new or underserved demographics through careful market research. And, ultimately, we provide recommendations and a detailed plan for follow-up actions.

This is a thirty-day audit and strategy formulation service priced at $10,000 and designed to analyze a brand's entire digital footprint to get a view of its current state and provide a clear path forward. The program includes several elements:

- **Site audit**: An assessment of the brand's website to assess the user experience (UX), flow patterns, natural funnels, and the checkout process for D2C sales. This includes an evaluation of SEO practices and how effectively the site is being indexed.

- **Social audit**: We take a look at the brand's social media channels, focusing on strategy, content quality, engagement, and reach. The audit looks at the impact of content over follower counts, with a focus on enhancing meaningful interactions with the brand's audience.

- **Brand audit**: A review of the brand's relevance, consistency, and current positioning in the market. This includes checking against existing brand guidelines to ensure alignment across all marketing efforts.

- **Competitive research**: An in-depth look at the brand's competitive landscape, including share of voice on social media and PR, as well as the digital marketing strategies being employed by competitors. This is critical for identifying both opportunities and threats in the market.

- **Digital marketing funnel analysis**: We take a look at both the brand and its competitors' digital marketing efforts, including paid search and social media advertising. This analysis helps identify potential inefficiencies, like bidding wars on keywords that could erode profit margins.

When our analysis is complete, we provide a clearly defined set of next steps in an action plan that can be implemented by the brand's internal team or with the assistance of our team. For many, though, the audit serves as the foundation for a long-term partnership with

Kahn Media, although again, there's no obligation to continue beyond the program.

One of the interesting things we've found, though, is that even though we provide a detailed road map, most brands quickly recognize the complexity of attempting to follow it themselves. PR in an era of digital marketing is rapidly changing. It can be challenging enough for an agency to stay on top of these changes—it can be virtually impossible for a brand to do the same.

By thoroughly evaluating your current approach and making the necessary adjustments, you can ensure that your PR and marketing efforts are not only aligned with your business goals but are also poised to deliver the measurable results that drive long-term success.

TAKEAWAYS

This chapter took a look at the critical role of strategic planning, measurement, and adaptation in achieving PR and marketing success. Consider the following questions to evaluate your approach to KPIs and measurement to ensure that your PR and marketing strategies are driving the results you're looking for.

→ How do your current KPIs align with your overarching business goals? Reflect on whether your KPIs were chosen to directly support your business objectives, like increasing brand awareness, boosting sales, or enhancing customer loyalty.

→ What processes do you have in place for regularly reviewing and adjusting your KPIs? Consider the mechanisms you use to assess the relevance and effectiveness of your KPIs over time, ensuring they remain aligned with evolving business goals and market conditions.

→ How effectively are you using data and analytics tools to measure PR and marketing efforts? Evaluate your use of tools like Google Analytics, Semrush, HubSpot, and others for tracking real-time data and gaining insights into audience behavior and campaign performance. Are they giving you the in-depth, 360-degree insights you need?

→ What challenges have you encountered in aligning KPIs with business goals? How have you addressed them?

→ Looking ahead, what new metrics might be relevant to your business goals, and how can you incorporate them into your measurement strategy?

CHAPTER 8

THE ROAD TO TOMORROW

(THE FUTURE OF PR/MEDIA)

Before we dive into the future of PR, let's take a look back at a situation that I think is very instructive and relevant for us here.

We have two agencies—one focused on outdoor recreation and one in automotive. Both are relatively small networks from a media or PR standpoint, and tight-knit groups. You get to know the people you work with well. I started my career as an editor and writer at Petersen Publishing, which was at the time the largest enthusiast magazine publisher in the world. After a few buyouts and private equity flips, it was rebranded and merged with a company that owned newsstands called Source Interlink. They had more than twenty automotive publications, including *Motor Trend*, *Hot Rod*, and the Transworld titles. The new company did well for a while, but they failed to understand how the internet would disrupt their model. Instead of leaning into it—as they had the brands, content, and authority to absolutely dominate the new medium—they saw the web as competition and decided to delay posting stories online until after the magazines had run them, often delaying stories from hitting sites by three to four months. As a result, they lost traffic, subscriptions, and eventually authority and ad dollars. They entered into Chapter 11 bankruptcy in 2009, ultimately causing them to shut down the operations of Source Interlink Distribution in 2014.

Then, in December 2019, they announced that they were shuttering nineteen of their twenty-two automotive magazines by year-end, continuing only with *MotorTrend*, *Hot Rod*, and *Four Wheeler*—just weeks before a big media trade conference for the automotive industry. The day it happened was a Black Monday like I had never seen in my career—hundreds and hundreds of people were laid off. Some of those who had been laid off still came to the show; many didn't. Those that did were walking around like the walking dead—just blindsided.

I wasn't entirely blindsided. I had predicted this was going to happen, just not in such an abrupt manner. I thought it was going to be a slow atrophy over a period of years. The cause of Source Interlink's demise was multifaceted, but one primary driver was the shift from traditional consumption of print media to the consumption of online magazines and the use of e-book readers.

Those who lost their jobs went in different directions. A small handful of the editors became content creators, doing content creation for brands, or maybe starting their own YouTube channels, but it wasn't many of them. A lot of them became realtors.

Another long-tail impact was a huge, and sudden, shift in marketing budgets of companies that devoted the majority of their marketing budgets to advertising in these magazines. Most of them set their budgets in November and December, and this happened in January. They didn't really know what to do.

We had a lot of clients approach us coming out of that situation saying, "We need help. What do we do?"

And then COVID-19 hit. Now we had complete disruption, and companies were worried about whether they were going to go out of business. And they were cutting their budgets because we were not sure if the world was ending. So now we had to help them run super lean and super targeted.

That wasn't the end of it. In early 2024, Warner Bros. Discovery announced that it was shifting programming from MotorTrend+ streaming service to Max and Discovery+ and shutting down the subscription offering. The company where I started my career less than a quarter century ago, at the time one of the biggest publishing companies (and authority marketing hubs with more than three dozen major titles) had essentially ceased to exist—all because the people in charge failed to plan for the future and act accordingly. Consumer tastes hadn't changed that much—fishing enthusiasts didn't stop fishing and still wanted to consume fishing content; Mustang fans still wanted to learn more about the parts and trends and new builds in the Mustang world—they just wanted a different delivery mechanism for the content, and the old Petersen/Source Interlink/Discovery team were late to the party, leaving brands to go their own way (with our help, in many cases).

A SEA SHIFT IN PAYMENT MODELS AND FOCUS

All these impacts just started piling up. Over the next couple of years, the PR industry was completely transformed. Before this, when I'd talk about PR and what it meant, I was actually talking about media relations. But, coming out of these experiences, PR suddenly became public relations where we're now talking to the consumer (the public). Maybe we're doing that through a blog, through a newsletter, through social channels, through the lens of an influencer or content creators, through digital marketing.

PR, MARKETING, AND BRANDING CONVERGE

It used to be that PR, marketing, and branding were three separate things that were handled through different agencies and different budgets. Suddenly, things started to merge. It was, I think, a huge game changer that redefined not only how we do business but how our industry does business.

As the print magazine business faltered, a lot of focus and dollars shifted to digital. Paper is just not as relevant, and the distribution channels aren't as prevalent as they used to be. As the internet emerged in the early days, print publishers transitioned their content to digital, but they still used the old print model. Even though the digital channel existed, they'd say, "We're not going to publish content until the magazine is on the newsstands," or maybe even off the newsstands. So, despite the new digital landscape, this still meant a three-to-four-month lag from when a story was written to when it showed up on the internet.

Then more nimble competition emerged.

VELOCITY AND TRAFFIC

Independent blogs became the primary source of information. Jason Katanas, for instance, had Weblogs Inc. and had a lot of different enthusiast blogs like Gadget. The Gawker Group had Gizmoto. There was TechCrunch and Vice. All of these were media sites owned by someone who said, "Hey, velocity and traffic are what we need now. We need to get stuff up and out as fast as we can."

Initially, these websites made their money through ads. They'd bring on a sponsor, run their ads, and rake in the cash based on page views. It was all about the CPM model—cost per one thousand impressions. The more page views a site had, the more impressions an ad would get, and the more money the site would make. It was a simple, understandable business model.

CONSOLIDATION AND PAYMENT SHIFTS

But then, things started to change. Many of these sites got bought out by private equity groups and rolled into new deals. These groups owned pretty much all the major media sites, except for the corporate-owned ones like CNN and Fox News. And with the arrival of these private equity groups, the business model shifted.

Instead of having an ad sales team, these sites started using ad stacks like Google's. These ad stacks would plug ads into a site based on the demographics of the readership. The site would get a share of the ad revenue, and Google would take a cut. The focus shifted from selling ads to driving traffic.

This shift had a big impact on the nature of the content. Instead of long, investigative pieces, we started seeing quick-hit listicles. These shorter articles could generate more clicks and, therefore, more ad revenue. It was a seismic shift in the media landscape, and it changed the way PR had to pitch stories. But the changes didn't stop there. As the economy shifted gears, these private-equity-owned media sites started to contract. Layoffs became common, and it became even harder to work with what was once considered traditional media.

Now, here's where things get interesting. In the mid-2020s, we're in the midst of a Copernican shift in marketing. Just as Copernicus realized that Earth wasn't the center of the solar system, marketers are realizing that their brand isn't the center of their marketing universe.

THE CUSTOMER BECOMES THE FOCUS

Customers don't want to go to your website. They want you to come to them. They want to find your product on Google or see it in their Instagram feed. They want a passive shopping experience, one that doesn't require them to leave the platform they're on.

This shift has huge implications for brands and advertisers. It means that the old ways of doing things aren't going to cut it anymore. It means that we need to rethink our strategies and find new ways to reach our customers.

And that brings us to influencers. These social media stars have a captive audience and the power to sway their followers' purchasing decisions. They're paid in a variety of ways, including gifts, sponsored posts, and partnerships. And they're incredibly effective at building trust and credibility for brands. But influencers are also "normal people" as we'll see.

So, as we look to the future of PR, we need to keep these changes in mind. We need to adapt to the shifting media landscape and find new ways to reach our customers. And most importantly, we need to remember that in this new marketing solar system, the customer is the sun, and we are all just planets in orbit.

In this environment what we're seeing is a shift to social and a greater focus on owned media.

A SHIFT TO SOCIAL

As opportunities for companies to get their messages out via traditional media have dwindled, brands have been forced to forge new pathways. The shift toward influencers and content creators has been not just a trend, but a necessity.

Similarly, the rise of social media as a dominant platform has provided a powerful tool to reach and engage directly with a massive audience—once only possible through traditional media outlets like TV, radio, and print. Doing this effectively requires paying attention to who's talking about you and how and responding quickly and authentically by engaging in conversations with consumers in digital environments.

STANLEY GETS IT RIGHT

An example of a brand that has really excelled in this environment is Stanley. Despite the fact that they're a hardware brand that's been around for more than one hundred years, they've been able to successfully shift their PR and communication practices to leverage the new digital environment and the power of social interactions. While they've done some PR, their efforts have been primarily focused on social content. They have a clear brand voice, and they just do a great job engaging with their audiences authentically.

Stanley is intentionally going after a young audience, focusing primarily on Instagram and TikTok with content that is fun and irreverent, but fact based. They're very clear about who they're talking to. And they're also very much on top of who's talking about them and engaging them with authenticity—and velocity.

So, there was a woman on TikTok, Danielle, whose car burned in a fire. She put up her own video that went viral organically. The Stanley connection? Well, despite the fact that her car was a total wreck, and she was obviously pretty upset about that, she went to her salvaged car to find her Stanley cup. Not only did the cup survive the fire, but there was still ice in the cup! The video was just in the moment, very low production value.

A day or two later, Stanley responded with their own video with similar production value that a staffer clearly shot of Stanley's global president, Terence Reilly, dressed very casually in an office setting, with Stanley cups in the background. He looked at the camera and said, "Wow, what an ordeal. We're all really glad you're safe. Thanks for sharing that video because wow, it really shows how Stanleys are built for life because of what it went through with you. I couldn't think of a better example of our products' quality. But, anyway, we're glad you're safe. I've seen a lot of comments that we should send you some Stanleys. Well, we're gonna send you some Stanleys. But there's one more thing. We've never done this before. And we'll probably never do it again. But we'd love to replace your vehicle. Yeah, all of us at Stanley. We'd really like to replace your vehicle. So, check your DMs for details. Thanks. Be safe. Cheers."[25]

This is an amazing illustration of how authenticity and velocity can create awareness and engagement and really impact brand value. In this case, the response was just off the rails. It was completely insane how much exposure this got—positive exposure. The cost of that car was nothing compared to the value of the exposure Stanley received. Not only the social exposure but, in addition, hundreds and hundreds of articles were written about it—not just in marketing and PR trade journals, but in outlets like *USA Today* and Yahoo News.

It worked because the response was quick (velocity), and it was authentic. It doesn't work as well when it's not. Below is another example.

---

25 "Stanley Travel Mug Survives Car Fire in Viral Video, Company Offers to Replace Vehicle," Complex, January 27, 2024, https://www.complex.com/life/a/backwoodsaltar/stanley-travel-mug-survives-car-fire-in-viral-video.

NORTH FACE FUMBLES

In this case, the brand is North Face. There was a young lady from Texas, Jenn, who was on vacation in New Zealand and hiking on top of a mountain where it was dumping rain. She was wearing a new North Face jacket that she bought specifically for the trip—and she was soaked through.

So, Jenn did what most young people today do in these situations. She took a video and posted it on TikTok and basically said, "Hey, North Face, you let me down here. The tag on this jacket says it's a rainproof rain jacket, and obviously, it's not." At the time she wasn't an influencer. She had a relatively small following.

North Face's response wasn't as quick as Stanley's, and this wasn't a positive situation. They were basically being called out on poor product quality. So, several days or a few weeks later, they finally get around to posting. And what they posted was a video—not just any video, but a highly produced, high production-value video that showed a North Face employee running out of an office building, grabbing a new raincoat off the rack, hopping into a helicopter, and flying to the top of a mountain. There, he handed the new jacket to the customer, who was now dry, fully made up, and looking like a supermodel. She smiled a million-dollar smile and said, "Thanks, North Face."[26]

The video got a lot of views, but the comments were mixed. Some viewers applauded North Face for the great content, while others questioned the authenticity of the video. Was it staged? Was the initial complaint real? Did they really fly her back to New Zealand? Despite the skepticism, the video did get mostly positive earned media, making

---

26   "The North Face Delivered Jacket via Helicopter in Viral TikTok Complaint,"
      Business Insider, December 2023, https://www.businessinsider.com/
      the-north-face-delivered-jacket-via-helicopter-viral-tiktok-complaint-2023-12.

it a win for North Face. But it raises an important question: Does it feel authentic? I don't think so.

What these two examples underscore is the importance of authenticity in PR and marketing. In the digital age, consumers are increasingly savvy. They can tell when a brand is being genuine and when it's putting on a show. Authenticity is key to successful PR and marketing efforts.

So, what does this mean for companies wanting to get great exposure in the new digital PR landscape?

PRACTICAL INSIGHTS FOR MAKING THE SHIFT TO DIGITAL

As these examples illustrate, transparency and honesty are paramount in this new digital media landscape where brands have both the opportunity and the mandate to speak directly to their consumers. The gatekeepers of the earned media environment no longer play as critical a role (although they're still there). But the opportunity to gain organic traction requires transparency and honesty.

In the new PR landscape, brands must be open, authentic, and provide value to consumers and their customers. They have the opportunity to use their own channels and relationships and to leverage their own events to reach their audiences by going to them where they live, on the platforms they use, and with the content they want to consume.

It's all about understanding the customer's preferences and delivering content that's authentic to their brands. In this environment brands need to do several things to remain relevant and top of mind.

Embrace the Shift to Digital

The shift to digital has transformed the PR landscape. Traditional media outlets have been replaced by digital platforms, and the focus has shifted from media relations to public relations. Brands are now communicating directly with the public through blogs, newsletters, social channels, and influencers. Digital marketing, even digital advertising, should feel like organic, authentic content that is relevant to the consumer.

Understand the Changing Media Landscape

The media landscape has changed dramatically over the years. Print publications have given way to digital platforms, and the focus has shifted from page views and ad impressions to creating engaging content. Brands need to understand these changes and adapt their PR strategies accordingly. For instance, giving an exclusive first look at a new product to a popular YouTuber can be more impactful than featuring it in a traditional media outlet.

Build Meaningful Relationships

In the digital age, building meaningful relationships with influencers and content creators is crucial. Understand your audience, your voice, and the theme of your channels. Be respectful of your audience's time and ensure your pitches are relevant to their needs and interests.

Avoid the "Spray and Pray" Approach

When pitching to traditional media outlets or influencers, understand that the "spray and pray" approach, where brands send out mass pitches hoping one will stick, is not effective in the digital age. In fact, as we've seen, that approach can also backfire. With the increase in the number of influencers and content creators, it's more important than ever to personalize your pitches. A poorly targeted, impersonal pitch will not only be ineffective but can also damage your relationship with the influencer—and your audience.

Leverage Newsjacking, but Do It Authentically

We've talked about newsjacking—using news and current events as a jumping-off point for your own messaging. It can work. But, as with PR and marketing communications, in general, it has to be authentic.

Even the big brands sometimes fail to get this right. A prime example is a Pepsi commercial from 2017. If you recall, that was a time when certain issues were starting to bubble to the surface of the news cycle. We were starting to hear stories of police brutality, particularly in African American communities. It was a time of rising tension, change, and a growing demand for social justice.

Pepsi attempted to join this conversation and make a statement by creating social commentary through an ad featuring Kendall Jenner, the billionaire, influencer, model, and celebrity. This could have been a simple ad with Kendall enjoying a Pepsi and talking about how great it tastes. But they decided to take this a step further. They wanted to blend their earned and owned media to create a social statement.

The ad started with Kendall on a photo shoot, taking a break, and sipping her Pepsi. She saw a protest for African American rights in the street and decided to join in. She walked off the set, joined the protest, and carried a sign down the street.

The spot was released on streaming services, YouTube, and television. But the reaction wasn't what they had anticipated or hoped for.

People found the spot to be inauthentic and off putting. They questioned how much Kendall earned from the commercial, which was several million dollars. They criticized the commercialization of a movement that was about human rights. And they suggested that if Kendall and Pepsi truly believed in the cause, they should go to a real protest or donate to organizations that were trying to move the cause forward.

The backlash came from all sides. Social justice advocates found it offensive because of its crass commercialization. Others just wanted to enjoy their soda without a side of judgment. They wanted Pepsi to focus on the taste of the product, not on social issues. Pepsi pulled the ad.

Ultimately, the ad was a big misstep for the brand. It was inauthentic, it was fake, it was crass commercialization. It was the exact opposite of what an effective ad or PR message should be. The only thing it succeeded at is offering a lesson about what not to do.

GENAI: THE GREAT UNKNOWN

Another major impact on the PR industry emerged in 2023, and that, as of the time of this writing, was still beginning to play out across the profession and, in truth, across all professions. Generative AI, or GenAI—technology that allows content including text, images, and video to be created with the click of a button.

In one of our all-hands meetings recently, a couple of our graphic designers were getting a little grumpy and complaining that they needed to be more involved in the creative process. After a while, I pulled out my phone and opened up DALL-E, a ChatGPT image generator that produces high-quality images based on descriptions you provide it via text. I gave it a prompt, and it cranked out a pretty good rendering of an image. I did that for free in about thirty seconds. It was a pretty awkward conversation.

But I'm having that same kind of conversation with clients now. I had a client proudly send me a press release the other day and said,

"Hey, check it out." I did, and it was pretty good. He created it with ChatGPT.

As some would tell it, GenAI will be the death of original content creation by human beings. And who knows? Maybe it will. But I'm not so sure. In fact, I remember similar concerns from when I was just cutting my teeth in the publishing world and film cameras were the norm. We shot everything on Chrome slide film because nothing beat its color saturation. You'd go out, shoot an assignment, and come back with a bag full of film canisters.

We had an off-site lab where we'd send our rolls of film, and then it was a waiting game. You'd pray to the photography gods, and a week or two later, you'd get boxes full of Chrome slides back. We'd huddle around the light table in the art department, sifting through each slide, looking for those ten out of a hundred shots that were pure gold. Those were the keepers, the ones that made the cut. But the process didn't end there. Those slides then had to be scanned, another hurdle to clear.

Then everything changed. I'll never forget that day. We had this meeting where we were all handed digital cameras. It was a mix of excitement and pure dread. Some of us thought it was the coolest thing ever while others were convinced it was the apocalypse for photography.

The early days of digital were rough. You couldn't use a digital image for a full magazine spread, for instance, without it looking pixelated. We had to adapt, change the way we shot. We started doing more verticals, and for those big spreads, we'd still rely on film. But the game changer was that we'd know—right then and there—how a shoot looked and if the shots were coming out well. The concept of waiting around days or weeks with bated breath to learn if your shoot was a success or a failure was over. Velocity and overall quality both improved overnight. The photographers who leaned into that pivot and evolved alongside their tech and gear became faster, more efficient and better. They went on to succeed. Those that refused to grow with these changes slowly faded away.

The transition from film to digital wasn't just about the technology. It was a mindset shift. We had to rethink our entire approach to photography. And now, look at us. Digital photography has come so far that you can snag a top-notch digital camera without breaking the bank, take a shot, and instantly see if it's a winner. You can beam that image straight to your phone, tweak it in an app like Lightroom with presets you've dialed in, and share it with thousands of fans in real time.

That's revolutionary. That's what GenAI will be.

The thing is that photography didn't die with the introduction of digital—it evolved. It got more accessible, more immediate, and, yes, easier in some ways. But the essence of photography—the eye for a shot, the composition, the storytelling—that's still on us.

That's the parallel I see with marketing and AI today. It's not that AI is taking over. It's about us using AI to elevate what we do, to tell our stories better and to connect more deeply. We're looking down the barrel of a rapidly evolving technological landscape. It's clear that AI is not just a passing fad but a seismic shift that's reshaping the industry. With giants like Google and Microsoft and visionaries like Elon Musk pouring billions of dollars into AI, we're on the cusp of a revolution that's set to redefine the very essence of PR.

But here's the thing. It's not and has never been about the tools. With AI the real magic will happen when we use it as a collaborator, not as a replacement. It's about what happens when we feed it our unique tone and voice, our audience insights, and let it amplify our creative capacity. AI can help us ideate, strategize, and even predict trends—but it's up to us to steer the ship and ensure the content we create is accurate, ethical, and genuinely engaging.

In PR, it's also up to us to build and maintain the kind of relationships that really give us traction. It's not just about writing a press release, which my client demonstrated he could do easily with ChatGPT. It's more about strategizing around the kind of exposure you're looking for and gaining that exposure based on the relationships you've established with reporters, journalists, influencers, and others. And, as we've seen, it's about having an entire strategy around how to use the right combination of owned, earned, and paid media to get the results you're looking for.

AI can't do that—yet.

In a world of CGI-backed superhero movies, there's a reason why movies like *Barbie* and *Oppenheimer* still do well. It's because there's a level of humanity there—they're telling more powerful stories in a very human way. In the meantime, Marvel just keeps cranking out the same movie over and over again with different costumes, and it all starts to blend together.

I have a feeling that's the same sort of thing we're going to see with AI-generated content whether we're talking words or visuals.

The evolution of AI in PR is bound to accelerate, we just don't know how yet. We'll see more sophisticated tools, more intuitive interfaces—and more ethical dilemmas. But even as the landscape shifts and even more sophisticated technology emerges, our core mission remains the same—to tell compelling stories, to build meaningful relationships, and to navigate the ever-changing tides of public opinion.

CHALLENGING, BUT ALSO EXCITING TIMES

It's a challenging time to be in PR, but it's also an exciting time.

For a long time, the North Star for companies was always the brand. Everything we did, from PR to marketing, was about doing what was right for the brand.

Take Southwest Airlines as an example. They were consistent, they knew who they were and who their customer was, and what their brand values were. They focused on being the best at what they could be, not trying to be anything else. They weren't trying to be a hotel business or a food service business. They were simply about getting people from point A to point B in a friendly, reliable, and affordable way. This focus permeated everything they did, from PR to marketing and advertising. But as founder and longtime CEO, Herb Kelleher, transitioned from CEO to chairman emeritus, the focus of the company began to wander, and upon his death in 2019, new leadership began aggressively growing the bottom line of the company by expanding into new markets, trying new types of marketing, and trying to compete with other airlines for total dominance. They lost their focus, and the KPIs changed. Instead of being the "friendly" airline with incredible customer service and affordable prices, Southwest tried to be everything to everyone, while failing to reinvest in people and upgraded systems to support customers.

This all came to a head in December 2022, when its computer system crashed just before Christmas, cancelling nearly seventeen thousand flights and stranding millions of people. If this had happened twenty years ago, there would have been stories on the evening news and in the papers, but they would have been fairly sterile third-person accounts of a technical snafu and the flights that were cancelled as a result. But today ... literally millions of people were posting videos of airport terminals packed with standing-room-only crowds as people were stranded overnight (or in some cases for days) trying to get home for the holidays. Children crying, families separated, even soldiers trying to get home to see their loved ones. The story was so much bigger than a story on the news; it was reality playing out in real time.

As a result, the goodwill and positive customer experience the company had built for half a century started to crack under the pressure. Southwest was compelled by the government to pay a record $140 million fine, but the PR crisis, drop in sales, and shocking 14 percent single-day stock price drop caused more damage than the fine itself. Company leaders are still trying to rebuild its reputation today.

The takeaway from this debacle? The velocity of modern content creation, curation, and distribution is like wildfire—it can be an incredible tool for growth, but it can also be a shockingly destructive force. So be aware of what you're getting into, have a plan, execute quickly, and be ready to act fast if things go well—or otherwise.

It's like the Wild West out there. We've got content creators, influencers, independent voices, and podcasters shaking things up. It's a shift back to the beginning, where independent voices ruled. The print industry is dying, and digital is taking over. It's all about driving traffic now, and the nature of how we pitch to outlets has changed. We're seeing a shift where the center of our solar system is not the brand or the website—but the customer.

And we're seeing the rapid emergence and adoption of GenAI.

So, what's the future of PR in this digital marketing era? It's about adapting to these changes, focusing on the customer, and finding new ways to connect with them. It's about realizing that the old ways of doing things might not work anymore, and that's okay. It's a new era. But it's also a very exciting time to be in PR and marketing.

As we chart our course through this new era, let's not lose sight of what makes PR truly impactful. It's not the tools we use, but the stories we tell and the connections we make—the relationships we build and maintain over time. AI is here to stay, and even more disruptive innovations are likely to continue to emerge, but it's up to us to harness its potential to elevate our craft, to adapt, evolve, and thrive in the future of PR.

TAKEAWAYS

The world of PR is changing rapidly. How well are you positioned to identify and navigate these changes to ensure your brand is future ready? This set of questions is examining how a brand/individual might be poised to meet the future. These placeholder questions can be replaced with questions that examine how well the reader's organization is poised to meet the future.

→ Does your current PR strategy demonstrate a balance between traditional media relations and direct-to-consumer engagement? What opportunities do you have to increase your direct contact with customers and potential customers?

→ How well are you leveraging digital channels to get your messages in front of broader audiences?

→ Are you engaged with any influencers? Could you be? What influencers in your area of market focus have the potential to positively influence your audience?

→ What steps can you take to ensure that your brand will remain future ready?

→ Is your organization poised to take advantage of an increased level of transparency?

→ Are you prepared to scale across multiple platforms?

→ Is there a plan for innovation in the face of changes in technology? Changes to audience needs?

CHAPTER 9

NAVIGATING THE NEXUS:

THE CONVERGENCE OF PR, MARKETING, AND TECHNOLOGY

*T*he public relations landscape is in a state of constant flux, evolving at an unprecedented pace. As we look back at the journey we've taken through the previous chapters, it becomes evident that the future of PR is not just about adapting to changes but about anticipating and leading them. This chapter delves into the critical convergence of PR, marketing, and technology, exploring how these fields are increasingly intertwined and what this means for the future of our industry.

THE BLURRING LINES BETWEEN PR AND MARKETING

In the past, PR and marketing operated in silos, each with its own distinct goals and strategies. PR was about building relationships and managing the brand's reputation, while marketing focused on driving sales and increasing market share. Today, these distinctions are becoming less clear. The integration of PR and marketing strategies is not just a trend but a necessity in the digital age.

Integrated campaigns: Successful brands now leverage integrated campaigns that combine PR, marketing, and advertising to create a unified message. For example, consider a product launch that uses traditional media coverage (earned media), social media promotions (owned media), and targeted ads (paid media). By coordinating these efforts, brands can amplify their reach and impact.

A prime example of this approach is the launch of Tesla's Model 3. Tesla didn't rely solely on traditional media to generate buzz. Instead, they created a multifaceted campaign that included Elon Musk's personal social media announcements, high-profile press events, and strategic partnerships with influencers in the tech and automotive industries. This approach not only garnered extensive media coverage but also created a viral buzz on social platforms, driving significant preorders before the car was even available.

Content strategy: Content is the linchpin of this integration. A well-crafted content strategy can serve multiple purposes—building brand awareness, engaging customers, and driving conversions. Brands like Red Bull have mastered this approach by creating compelling content that resonates with their audience and reinforces their brand identity.

Red Bull's "Stratos" project is a classic example. By sponsoring and publicizing Felix Baumgartner's record-breaking free fall from the edge of space, Red Bull created content that was thrilling, shareable, and closely aligned with their brand's extreme sports image. The event was broadcast live, generating millions of views, and the content was repurposed across various platforms, ensuring prolonged engagement. This not only enhanced Red Bull's brand visibility but also cemented its reputation as a leader in extreme sports.

THE ROLE OF TECHNOLOGY IN MODERN PR

Technology is reshaping the PR landscape in profound ways. From AI-powered analytics to sophisticated CRM systems, technological advancements are providing PR professionals with new tools to enhance their strategies and measure their impact.

AI and automation: AI is revolutionizing PR by automating routine tasks, providing insights through data analysis, and even generating content. Tools like AI-driven media monitoring can track brand mentions in real time, analyze sentiment, and provide actionable insights. Chatbots and virtual assistants can handle customer inquiries, allowing PR teams to focus on more strategic tasks.

Take Coca-Cola, for example. The brand uses AI to analyze social media conversations in real time, gaining insights into consumer sentiment and preferences. This data allows Coca-Cola to tailor its marketing campaigns to better resonate with its audience. Additionally, AI-powered chatbots on their website and social media platforms provide instant customer service, enhancing user experience and engagement.

Data analytics: Data is the new currency in PR. Advanced analytics tools enable PR professionals to measure the effectiveness of their campaigns with precision. Metrics such as engagement rates, click-through rates, and conversion rates provide a clear picture of what's working and what's not. This data-driven approach allows for continuous optimization and more informed decision-making.

Netflix exemplifies the power of data analytics. By analyzing viewer data, Netflix can predict what content will be popular and make informed decisions about which shows to produce. This data-driven strategy has led to the creation of hit series like *Stranger Things* and *The Crown*, which have not only attracted new subscribers but also generated extensive media coverage and social media buzz.

Digital storytelling: The rise of digital platforms has transformed the way stories are told. Brands can now use multimedia content— videos, podcasts, interactive infographics—to engage their audience in more immersive ways. Virtual reality (VR) and augmented reality (AR) are also emerging as powerful tools for storytelling, offering unique and memorable experiences.

National Geographic's use of VR to document the experiences of endangered species is a compelling example. By creating immersive VR experiences, National Geographic allows viewers to step into the world of these animals, fostering a deeper emotional connection and driving home the importance of conservation. This innovative approach not only educates but also engages viewers in a powerful way.

AGILITY AND ADAPTABILITY: KEYS TO FUTURE SUCCESS

In an era of rapid technological advancement and shifting consumer preferences, agility and adaptability are crucial for success. Brands must be able to pivot quickly, embrace new technologies, and stay ahead of trends.

Agile PR strategies: Agile methodologies, which originated in the software development world, are now being applied to PR. Agile PR involves iterative planning, constant feedback, and the ability to adjust strategies on the fly. This approach allows PR teams to respond to real-time events and capitalize on emerging opportunities.

For instance, during the COVID-19 pandemic, many companies had to rapidly adjust their PR strategies. Zoom, the video conferencing platform, quickly pivoted its messaging to address the sudden increase in remote work and virtual socializing. They launched new features, increased security measures, and communicated these changes effectively through various channels. This agile response not only addressed immediate concerns but also positioned Zoom as a leader in the new normal of remote communication.

Continuous learning: The pace of change in the PR industry means that continuous learning is essential. PR professionals must stay updated on the latest tools, techniques, and trends. This can be achieved through ongoing education, attending industry conferences, and participating in professional networks.

Salesforce provides an excellent example of fostering a culture of continuous learning. Through its online platform, Trailhead, Salesforce offers a variety of courses and certifications for its employees. This commitment to education ensures that their team stays ahead of industry trends and technological advancements, maintaining their competitive edge.

THE HUMAN ELEMENT IN A TECH-DRIVEN WORLD

While technology offers powerful tools for PR, the human element remains irreplaceable. Building relationships, understanding human emotions, and crafting authentic messages require a human touch.

Empathy and authenticity: In a world dominated by digital interactions, empathy and authenticity stand out. Brands that show genuine concern for their customers and communicate honestly are more likely to build lasting relationships. This is where the human element shines—understanding the nuances of human behavior and crafting messages that resonate on an emotional level.

Patagonia is a brand that exemplifies empathy and authenticity. Their commitment to environmental causes is not just a marketing ploy but a core part of their identity. Patagonia's "Don't Buy This Jacket" campaign encouraged consumers to think about the environmental impact of their purchases, fostering a deeper connection with their audience based on shared values. This authentic approach has built a loyal customer base and positioned Patagonia as a leader in sustainable business practices.

Ethical considerations: As technology becomes more integrated into PR, ethical considerations come to the forefront. Issues such as data privacy, transparency, and the responsible use of AI must be addressed. PR professionals have a responsibility to uphold ethical standards and ensure that their practices build trust rather than erode it.

Apple's stance on user privacy is a noteworthy example. By prioritizing customer data protection and being transparent about their data practices, Apple has built a reputation for trustworthiness. Their commitment to privacy has not only set them apart in the tech industry but also reinforced their brand's integrity.

CASE STUDY: STANLEY—A TRADITIONAL BRAND REINVENTS ITSELF

Stanley, known for its iconic green thermos, was traditionally seen as a rugged brand for outdoorsmen. However, they have successfully transformed their image to appeal to a younger, more diverse audience, particularly millennial and Gen Z females. This transformation is a testament to the power of integrating PR, marketing, and technology, particularly through social media and influencer marketing.

Strategic shift: Recognizing the potential of social media, Stanley shifted its focus to platforms like TikTok and Instagram. They collaborated with influencers who resonated with younger audiences, positioning their Stanley mug as a must-have accessory. Influencers showcased the mug in various settings—from yoga sessions to beach outings—highlighting its versatility and appeal.

One notable campaign involved influencers creating TikTok videos featuring the Stanley mug in their daily routines. The content was authentic and relatable, showcasing the mug not just as a product but as an integral part of their lifestyle. This strategy helped Stanley tap into the aspirational desires of young consumers, turning their mug into a symbol of a chic, active lifestyle.

Community engagement: Stanley didn't stop at influencer marketing. They also invested in corporate social responsibility (CSR) initiatives and community engagement. One particularly impactful story involves a TikTok video posted by a young woman whose car caught fire. Remarkably, her Stanley mug survived the blaze, and the ice inside was still frozen.

As detailed in chapter 8, Stanley's president, Terence Reilly, responded swiftly and authentically. He posted a video acknowledging the woman's hardship, expressing relief that she was safe, and thanking her for sharing her story. He then went a step further, offering to replace both her Stanley mug and her car. This heartfelt response was not only genuine but also resonated deeply with their audience.

Follow-up campaign: Stanley followed up with additional content, showing the young woman receiving her new car and mug. This follow-up reinforced their commitment to their customers and demonstrated the durability and reliability of their products. The campaign was a massive hit, generating extensive media coverage and social media buzz.

Sales soared, with a triple-digit increase over two years. This success underscores the importance of authenticity, empathy, and community engagement in modern PR and marketing.

CONCLUSION: THE FUTURE OF PR

The future of PR lies in its ability to adapt and innovate. The convergence of PR, marketing, and technology offers unprecedented opportunities to connect with audiences in meaningful ways. By embracing technology, staying agile, and maintaining a human touch, PR professionals can navigate this dynamic landscape and lead their brands to new heights.

Embrace technology without losing the human touch. Technology can enhance PR efforts, but the core of PR is about people. Use technology to streamline processes and gather insights, but ensure your communications remain personal and empathetic.

Focus on data-driven decision-making. Utilize data analytics to inform your strategies. Track campaign performance, analyze data, and use these insights to continuously optimize your efforts.

Stay agile and adaptable. The PR landscape is dynamic, and being able to pivot quickly is crucial. Adopt agile methodologies to respond to real-time events and emerging opportunities effectively.

Build strong relationships. Building and maintaining strong relationships with influencers, journalists, and your audience is key. Authenticity and trust are the foundations of these relationships.

Invest in continuous learning. The pace of change in PR means that staying updated on the latest tools, techniques, and trends is essential. Encourage continuous learning and professional development within your team.

Prioritize ethical practices. As technology becomes more integrated into PR, ensure your practices are ethical. Transparency, honesty, and respect for privacy are paramount.

Leverage multichannel strategies. Use a mix of earned, owned, and paid media to reach your audience effectively. Ensure your messaging is consistent across all channels.

Innovate with content. Experiment with different content formats—videos, podcasts, infographics—and leverage emerging technologies like AR and VR to create engaging and memorable experiences for your audience.

By adopting these strategies, PR professionals can navigate the convergence of PR, marketing, and technology, creating impactful and meaningful connections with their audiences.

FINAL THOUGHTS

The future of PR is bright, filled with opportunities for those willing to embrace change and innovate. The convergence of PR, marketing, and technology presents a unique chance to redefine how we connect with our audiences, build our brands, and drive success. By staying agile, leveraging technology, and maintaining a human-centered approach, we can navigate this exciting landscape and lead our brands to new heights.

As we chart our course through this new era, let's not lose sight of what makes PR truly impactful. It's not the tools we use, but the stories we tell and the connections we make. It's about building trust, fostering relationships, and creating a positive impact on the world around us. The future of PR is not just about adapting to change—it's about leading it.

TAKEAWAYS

It's important to invest effort into building genuine, respectful relationships with journalists by understanding their needs and providing real value for their audiences.

➡ Before pitching, thoroughly research the journalist, the stories they cover, their audience, and their preferences to ensure your pitch is highly relevant.

➡ Provide unique, timely story ideas that will captivate the journalist's audience. Press releases and direct pitches are still top sources for story ideas.

➡ Include multimedia elements like images, data visualizations/infographics, and videos with your pitches to bring stories to life.

➡ Provide original research, data on industry/market trends, and credible sources to bolster reporting and maintain audience trust.

➡ Craft pitches that are easily shareable on social media, where most journalists promote their work.

➡ Don't spam with irrelevant pitches, provide inaccurate information, make pitches sound like marketing, follow up excessively, or lack transparency.

CHAPTER 10

NAVIGATING ROUGH TERRAIN:

CRISIS COMMUNICATION AND REPUTATION MANAGEMENT

Navigating a crisis in the world of public relations is akin to driving on a treacherous mountain road. It requires a firm grip on the wheel, a clear view of the path ahead, and the ability to make quick, informed decisions to avoid pitfalls. Crisis communication and reputation management are integral components of a PR professional's toolkit. How a brand handles a crisis can make or break its reputation, and effective crisis communication strategies are essential for steering through rough terrain.

UNDERSTANDING CRISIS COMMUNICATION

Crisis communication involves the collection, processing, and dissemination of information required to address a crisis situation. It's about managing the message, maintaining transparency, and ensuring that all stakeholders are kept informed. The goal is to minimize damage, preserve trust, and emerge from the crisis stronger.

The Importance of Preparation

Preparation is the cornerstone of effective crisis communication. Brands must have a crisis communication plan in place long before any signs of trouble appear. This plan should outline the roles and responsibilities of the crisis management team, establish protocols for internal and external communication, and include predrafted templates for various scenarios.

A well-prepared brand can respond swiftly and effectively, maintaining control over the narrative and reducing the risk of misinformation spreading. As Benjamin Franklin famously said, "By failing to prepare, you are preparing to fail."

Crafting a Crisis Communication Plan

A comprehensive crisis communication plan should include the following elements:

Crisis management team: Identify key personnel who will be responsible for managing the crisis. This team should include representatives from PR, legal, HR, and senior management. Each member should have clearly defined roles and responsibilities.

Risk assessment: Conduct a thorough risk assessment to identify potential crisis scenarios. This can include product recalls, data breaches, legal issues, or negative publicity. Understanding potential risks allows the team to prepare appropriate responses.

Communication protocols: Establish clear protocols for internal and external communication. Determine how information will be disseminated to employees, stakeholders, customers, and the media. Ensure that all communication is consistent and aligned with the brand's values.

Predrafted statements: Prepare predrafted statements for various crisis scenarios. These templates can be customized quickly to address the specific situation, ensuring a prompt and accurate response.

Monitoring and evaluation: Implement a system for monitoring the situation in real time. This can include social media monitoring, media tracking, and feedback from customers and stakeholders. Regular evaluation allows for adjustments to the communication strategy as needed.

RESPONDING TO A CRISIS

When a crisis hits, the initial response is critical. The first twenty-four hours can set the tone for how the situation will unfold. It's essential to act quickly, communicate transparently, and demonstrate empathy.

The Golden Hour

The "golden hour" refers to the crucial first hour following a crisis. During this time, the crisis management team should gather all available information, assess the situation, and begin communicating with key stakeholders. Speed is of the essence, but so is accuracy. Rushing to respond without adequate information can lead to missteps and further damage.

Key Principles of Crisis Communication

Transparency, consistency, empathy, action, and follow-up are key principles in crisis communication. Being transparent means being open and honest about the situation. Acknowledge the issue, take responsibility, and provide as much information as possible. Transparency builds trust and credibility. Consistency ensures that all communication is aligned across all channels, preventing mixed messages that can create confusion and erode trust. Showing empathy humanizes the brand and demonstrates genuine concern for those affected by the crisis. Action outlines the steps being taken to address the crisis and prevent a recurrence, demonstrating accountability and commitment. Follow-up keeps stakeholders informed with regular updates, showing progress in resolving the issue.

CASE STUDY: STANLEY AND THE TIKTOK TRANSFORMATION

A prime example of effective crisis communication and reputation management is the story of Stanley, a brand known for its iconic camping thermoses, as we discussed in chapter 8. Stanley successfully transformed its image and became a much-desired brand for millennials and Gen Z females, primarily through TikTok and Instagram influencer marketing.

The Crisis: A Car Fire and a Resilient Mug

One incident that showcased Stanley's adept crisis management was a TikTok video posted by a young woman whose car had caught fire. Despite the devastation, her Stanley mug survived the blaze, and the ice in her drink remained frozen. The video quickly went viral, capturing the attention of millions.

The Response: Authenticity and Empathy

Stanley's president, Terence Reilly, saw the video and decided to respond personally. In a heartfelt video described in chapter 8, he apologized for the woman's hardship, thanked her for sharing the story, and offered to replace both her Stanley mug and her car. This gesture was not only generous but also demonstrated the brand's commitment to its customers.

The Follow-up: Leveraging the Story

Stanley didn't stop there. Weeks later, they followed up with more content showing the young woman with her brand-new car and a new Stanley mug. This content was shared on both Stanley's channel and the woman's, further amplifying the positive message.

The Result: A Brand Revitalized

The response was a smash hit. Stanley's sales surged, with triple-digit growth over two years. The brand's authenticity, empathy, and timely response transformed a potential crisis into a powerful marketing opportunity.

CRISIS COMMUNICATION IN THE DIGITAL AGE

The digital age has transformed crisis communication. Social media platforms allow for real-time communication, but they also amplify the speed and reach of a crisis. Brands must be prepared to respond swiftly and effectively across multiple channels.

The Role of Social Media

Social media is both a blessing and a curse in crisis communication. On one hand, it provides a platform for immediate communication with stakeholders. On the other hand, it can quickly spread negative information, making it difficult to control the narrative.

To navigate this terrain, brands must take the following actions:

Monitor social media. Use social media monitoring tools to track mentions, comments, and sentiment. This allows the crisis management team to respond quickly to emerging issues.

Engage with stakeholders. Engage with stakeholders in a timely and authentic manner. Respond to comments, answer questions, and provide updates. This demonstrates that the brand is attentive and responsive.

Control the narrative. Use social media to control the narrative by providing accurate and timely information. This can help counteract misinformation and rumors.

Leverage influencers. Collaborate with influencers to amplify positive messages and demonstrate third-party validation. Influencers can play a crucial role in shaping public perception.

BUILDING RESILIENCE: LONG-TERM REPUTATION MANAGEMENT

Crisis communication is not just about managing a single event; it's about building long-term resilience. Reputation management involves continuously nurturing and protecting the brand's image.

Proactive Reputation Management

Proactive reputation management involves taking these steps to build a positive brand image and mitigate potential risks:

Building trust: Consistently deliver on promises and maintain high standards of quality and service. Trust is the foundation of a strong reputation.

Engaging with stakeholders: Regularly engage with stakeholders through various channels. This includes customers, employees, investors, and the community. Building strong relationships can provide a buffer during a crisis.

Demonstrating corporate social responsibility (CSR): Implement CSR initiatives that align with the brand's values. CSR activities demonstrate the brand's commitment to social and environmental responsibility.

Ensuring transparent communication: Maintain transparency in all communication. Be open about the brand's practices, policies, and challenges. Transparency fosters trust and credibility.

CASE STUDY: JOHNSON & JOHNSON'S TYLENOL CRISIS

One of the most well-known examples of effective crisis communication is Johnson & Johnson's handling of the Tylenol crisis in 1982. This case study provides valuable lessons in crisis management and reputation restoration.

The Crisis: Product Tampering

In 1982, seven people in Chicago died after consuming Tylenol capsules that had been laced with cyanide. The crisis sparked nationwide fear and uncertainty, leading to a significant drop in sales and a damaged reputation for Johnson & Johnson.[27]

---

27   "James Lewis, the Suspect in the Deadly 1982 Tylenol Poisonings, Dies," *NPR*, July 10, 2023, https://www.npr.org/2023/07/10/1186906874/ james-lewis-suspect-tylenol-poisonings-dies.

The Response: Swift and Decisive Action

Johnson & Johnson's response was swift and decisive. The company immediately recalled 31 million bottles of Tylenol from store shelves, at a cost of over $100 million. They also halted all production and advertising of the product.

The company's CEO, James Burke, took a proactive approach, communicating openly with the public and the media. He emphasized the company's commitment to consumer safety and outlined the steps being taken to address the crisis. Burke's transparency and decisive action were pivotal in restoring trust and confidence in the brand.

The Aftermath: Long-term Reputation Management

Johnson & Johnson didn't just stop at managing the immediate crisis. They implemented several long-term measures to ensure such an incident wouldn't occur again. They introduced tamper-evident packaging, which became a new industry standard, and heavily invested in public education campaigns about product safety. The company's commitment to safety and transparency helped to not only recover its reputation but also to strengthen it. Today, Johnson & Johnson's response to the Tylenol crisis is often cited as a textbook example of effective crisis management.

NAVIGATING THE NEW MEDIA LANDSCAPE

The media landscape has evolved dramatically, influenced by the rapid pace of technological advancements and the rise of social media. In this dynamic environment, brands must be agile and innovative in their crisis communication strategies.

Real-Time Response

In today's digital age, information travels at lightning speed. Social media platforms like Twitter, Facebook, and Instagram can spread news (both good and bad) in a matter of seconds. Brands must be equipped to respond in real time to manage the narrative effectively.

For instance, in 2017, a United Airlines passenger was forcibly removed from an overbooked flight. The incident was captured on video and quickly went viral, sparking outrage worldwide. United's initial response was slow and tone deaf, focusing on company policies rather than expressing empathy for the passenger. This only fueled the backlash. It was only after the CEO issued a more sincere and empathetic apology that the situation began to stabilize. The lesson here is clear: in a crisis, timely and empathetic communication is crucial.

Social Media Monitoring and Engagement

Effective crisis communication in the digital age involves vigilant social media monitoring and proactive engagement. Brands must continuously track social media mentions, comments, and sentiment to identify potential issues before they escalate. Tools like Hootsuite, Brandwatch, and Sprout Social can help in monitoring social media activity in real time.

THE ROLE OF INFLUENCERS IN CRISIS COMMUNICATION

Influencers can play a critical role in crisis communication. Their established credibility and large following can help amplify a brand's message and restore public trust.

Leveraging Influencers

During a crisis, collaborating with influencers who align with the brand's values can be highly effective. Influencers can provide a third-party endorsement, which can be more persuasive than a brand's own statements. They can help humanize the brand, share positive stories, and reassure their followers about the brand's commitment to resolving the crisis.

Authenticity and Transparency

When leveraging influencers, authenticity and transparency are paramount. Influencers should genuinely believe in the brand and its values. Any perception of inauthenticity can backfire, further damaging the brand's reputation.

The Fyre Festival's disastrous failure in 2017 is a cautionary tale. The festival was heavily promoted by high-profile influencers like Kendall Jenner and Bella Hadid. However, when the event turned out to be a complete disaster, the backlash was not only directed at the organizers but also at the influencers who had promoted it without transparency about their compensation and involvement. This incident underscores the importance of authenticity and transparency in influencer partnerships.

BUILDING RESILIENCE THROUGH CORPORATE SOCIAL RESPONSIBILITY (CSR)

Corporate social responsibility (CSR) can be a powerful tool in building resilience and managing reputation, especially during a crisis. CSR initiatives demonstrate a brand's commitment to ethical practices, social good, and community engagement.

CSR as a Buffer

CSR activities can serve as a buffer during a crisis by showcasing the brand's positive impact and reinforcing its values. When a brand is known for its commitment to social and environmental causes, it can help mitigate negative perceptions during a crisis.

For instance, Patagonia, the outdoor clothing brand, is renowned for its strong commitment to environmental sustainability. When the company faced a potential boycott over a trademark dispute with another outdoor retailer, their longstanding reputation for ethical practices and environmental advocacy helped to diffuse the situation. Customers were more inclined to give Patagonia the benefit of the doubt due to its positive track record.

Communicating CSR Efforts

Effective communication of CSR efforts is crucial. Brands should highlight their CSR activities through various channels, including social media, press releases, and community events. This not only builds goodwill but also provides positive content that can be leveraged during a crisis.

NAVIGATING FUTURE CRISES

As we look to the future, it's clear that the landscape of crisis communication will continue to evolve. Brands must stay ahead of emerging trends and technologies to effectively manage crises and protect their reputations.

Embracing New Technologies

New technologies, such as artificial intelligence (AI) and big data analytics, offer significant opportunities for enhancing crisis communication. AI can help predict potential crises by analyzing vast amounts of data and identifying patterns. Big data analytics can provide real-time insights into public sentiment, enabling brands to respond more effectively.

For example, AI-powered sentiment-analysis tools can analyze social media posts, news articles, and customer feedback to gauge public sentiment. This can help brands identify emerging issues and address them proactively before they escalate into full-blown crises.

Preparing for the Unknown

The COVID-19 pandemic highlighted the importance of being prepared for the unknown. Brands must develop flexible crisis communication plans that can be adapted to a wide range of scenarios. This includes planning for global crises, such as pandemics, natural disasters, and geopolitical events, as well as more localized issues.

For instance, during the early days of the pandemic, many brands had to pivot quickly to address supply chain disruptions, shifts in consumer behavior, and health and safety concerns. Those with flexible crisis communication plans were better equipped to navigate these challenges and maintain their reputations.

THE ROAD TO REPUTATION RESILIENCE

Navigating rough terrain in crisis communication and reputation management requires a combination of preparation, agility, and empathy. Brands must be proactive in their crisis planning, transparent in their communication, and genuine in their interactions with stakeholders.

The lessons from Stanley, Johnson & Johnson, United Airlines, and other brands highlight the importance of swift, transparent, and empathetic communication. By embracing new technologies, leveraging the power of social media, and building long-term resilience through CSR, brands can not only survive crises but also emerge stronger.

As we continue to navigate the evolving landscape of public relations, one thing remains constant: the importance of trust. Trust is the foundation of a strong reputation, and it is built through consistent, transparent, and empathetic communication. By staying true to these principles, brands can navigate even the roughest terrain and continue to thrive.

By reflecting on the following questions, you can better prepare your brand to navigate the rough terrain of crisis communication and reputation management, ensuring long-term success and resilience.

TAKEAWAYS

→ **Crisis preparation**: Do you have a comprehensive crisis communication plan in place? How often do you review and update it?

→ **Crisis management team**: Have you identified key personnel for your crisis management team? Are their roles and responsibilities clearly defined?

→ **Risk assessment**: Have you conducted a thorough risk assessment to identify potential crisis scenarios relevant to your brand?

→ **Communication protocols**: Are your communication protocols for internal and external stakeholders well established and clearly documented?

➔ **Social media monitoring**: Do you use social media monitoring tools to track mentions, comments, and sentiment in real time?

➔ **Stakeholder engagement**: How effectively do you engage with stakeholders during a crisis? Do you respond to comments, answer questions, and provide updates promptly?

➔ **Transparency and empathy**: Are your crisis communication efforts characterized by transparency and empathy? Do you acknowledge issues and take responsibility?

➔ **Influencer collaboration**: Have you established relationships with influencers who align with your brand values? How can you leverage their credibility during a crisis?

➔ **CSR initiatives**: Are your CSR initiatives well communicated and aligned with your brand values? How do they contribute to building long-term resilience?

➔ **Technological adoption**: How well are you leveraging new technologies such as AI and big data analytics to enhance your crisis communication efforts?

➔ **Flexibility**: Is your crisis communication plan flexible enough to adapt to a wide range of scenarios, including global crises and localized issues?

➔ **Continuous improvement**: How regularly do you evaluate and refine your crisis communication strategies? Are you learning from past experiences and staying ahead of emerging trends?

HIGHWAY RESCUE

There's so much change and related confusion in the world of PR and marketing these days, which really points to the value of working with an agency that not only has experience but also stays up to date on these trends and shifts. A recent call from a reporter illustrated this. She was a nice young lady, fairly new to the job, and she just wouldn't let go of this question: "What do you say to people who are being replaced by AI in marketing and PR?" I told her, "I'm not sure that's happening."

She then rephrased the question, asking again, "How should agencies respond when they're getting calls from clients—are clients firing agencies because they have access to AI?" And again, I said, "I'm pretty hooked up in my industry, and I have yet to meet someone who's had that conversation." Finally, she gave it up.

DISRUPTION? YES. ANNIHILATION? NO.

Is AI a disruptor? Yes. If you're in a very specific role, it can help make things smoother and run faster. But will it replace a creative copywriter or someone who's a great photographer? No. Absolutely not. At least not yet.

I'm sure at some point the tools will get better. But right now, they're still pretty raw. It's easy to tell whether an image or copy has been created using ChatGPT or some other tool. It's all vanilla—or the imagery is so outrageous that it's obvious it's not real. If you're a copywriter, publicist, or journalist, you need to appeal to people either intellectually or emotionally, or they're not going to read your copy. Even if the tools could do that well right now, you still need someone at the controls creating the strategy and providing direction.

Actually, the situation now is that there are potentially more people out there creating content on behalf of a brand or a company than ever before. There might be fewer traditional salaried journalists sitting in a newsroom, but if you're adding in YouTubers, TikTokers, Instagram influencers, people with Substack newsletters, and podcasters, you'll see there are probably more "citizen journalists" out there making content than ever before in human history.

As in the story about the advent of digital photography I shared in chapter 8, AI isn't going to "replace" the role of marketing and PR, but it will be a tool that increases efficiency as a force multiplier. Where a group used to need several full-time or contract copywriters and copyeditors, AI can either empower one person to fill all those roles or—for those willing to push boundaries—it could allow all those people to be more efficient and increase their workload and effectiveness so the company can scale and grow by doing more/new things. Writing a prompt asking AI to build a marketing plan and then execute it won't result in anything *new*. That's what humans are great at—new ideas that make people stop, think, feel, and act. We'll need people to do that as long as we're still free of the Matrix. But will this tool, like digital cameras and Photoshop and every other leap in technology, make us more efficient and—dare I say it—better? I hope so.

From what I've seen, I think there's more opportunity now than ever before to work with an agency—if it's a good agency—and they're out there trying to figure out what the next thing is and how to connect brands with consumers through whatever methodology is likely to generate the most traction.

THE VALUE OF WORKING WITH AN AGENCY

Public relations, as we've seen, is more public than it's ever been before. It's less media relations and more public relations, and that's a harder job. It's herding cats at this point because there are so many potential ways to get your message out to your audience through owned, earned, and paid media.

Years ago, if you were in a niche industry—say you were in automotive aftermarket, or outdoor, or fashion—you could, in theory, build an internal team that would be able to do a pretty good job. Ten to twenty years ago, there might have been only eight publications reaching the right automotive B2B markets. You could hire a few people and sort out, internally, how to curate those relationships, write those releases, and create turnkey content—and you could probably do that without an agency.

It's a lot harder now. You need the breadth and depth that a larger team can provide.

THE POWER OF PARTNERING
WITH PR PROFESSIONALS

PR industry challenges have grown significantly over the past several years. The landscape is ever changing, and the need for a comprehensive—yet flexible—strategy is more critical than ever. Even larger organizations with in-house PR staff struggle to stay up to date on technology changes, new channels, new players requiring them to build new relationships, and constantly emerging competition.

Through my experience with Kahn Media, I've seen firsthand the transformative power an agency can have on a brand's narrative and its ability to connect with and influence an audience. It's not just about broadcasting messages—it's about starting conversations that lead to relationships, driving awareness, interest, preference, and demand.

Working with a PR and marketing agency can provide enormous benefits for brands, no matter how large they are or what industry they're in. Agencies like Kahn Media can help brands define clear brand messages and goals, create content that aligns with that narrative, and establish direct discourse and conversations with media and the direct consumer audience.

LEVERAGING EXISTING RELATIONSHIPS
AND CREATING NEW ONES

One of the key advantages of working with an agency is their ability to leverage their existing relationships to help brands reach a wider audience and gain more visibility with their target audiences. Agencies also have deep experience in creating content of all kinds—print, video, events, experiential interactions leveraging new media, and more.

Agencies are experts at gauging audience responses and tracking metrics to improve performance over time based on data-driven analysis of what's working, what's not, and areas of opportunity for improvement.

A key strength of an agency partnership is the ability to create and deliver integrated marketing strategies, leveraging the power of the broad array of traditional and digital communication channels to ensure a cohesive and brand-supportive dialogue.

REPUTATION AND CRISIS MANAGEMENT

Agencies are also there when brands need help with reputation and crisis management. When crises strike, and they inevitably do, having a partner who understands how to navigate these rough terrains can be the difference between a minor hiccup and a major disaster.

Consider the example of Stanley, the venerable brand known for its durable mugs and thermoses. Stanley was a household name for decades, primarily recognized for its rugged, reliable products favored by campers and outdoorsmen. But the company faced a challenge: how to reinvent itself for a new generation, particularly Millennials and Gen Z, who had different values and different expectations from the brands they supported.

STANLEY'S TRANSFORMATION THROUGH STRATEGIC PR AND CSR

Leadership at Stanley decided to transform the brand's image through a series of strategic PR moves, influencer partnerships, and a strong focus on corporate social responsibility (CSR). They aimed to make Stanley's products the must-have accessory for young women, primarily through platforms like TikTok and Instagram.

The pivotal moment came when the president of Stanley saw a TikTok video of a young woman who had used one of their mugs before a car fire. The car was completely destroyed, but the Stanley mug survived, with ice still frozen in her drink. The video went viral, capturing the attention of millions.

Seizing the moment, Stanley's president posted a heartfelt response. He expressed sympathy for her hardship, thanked her for sharing the video, and offered to replace both her Stanley mug and her car. This act of generosity was followed by weeks of content showing the young woman with her brand-new car and Stanley mug, shared across both her channel and Stanley's.

This campaign was a smash hit. It wasn't just about the products; it was about the story, the engagement, and the authenticity of the response. Sales skyrocketed, with triple-digit growth over a two-year period. This example underscores the power of timely, genuine responses and the impact of integrating CSR into your PR strategy.

THE POWER OF STORYTELLING IN PR

Storytelling is at the heart of effective PR. It's not just about presenting facts; it's about crafting narratives that resonate with your audience on a deeper level. The Stanley story is a prime example of this. The narrative wasn't just about a product surviving a fire; it was about resilience, generosity, and the human connection.

Another example that illustrates this point is our work with Lotus Cars. Lotus had a rich history but needed to reach new audiences and media. We managed the launch and press evaluation drives of the Evora GT, generating positive coverage within the automotive industry and beyond. We organized a multiday press event and loaned cars to key influencers and content creators, and the result was a surge in demand for the Lotus Evora GT.

RINGBROTHERS: FROM TRADITIONAL TO DIGITAL SUCCESS

Similarly, our work with Ringbrothers, a premium billet parts manufacturer and world-class custom car builder, showcases the power of integrating traditional public relations with modern digital strategies. Over a decade ago, when we started with the company, we built a social media presence for them, created unique content using their stunning automotive creations, and produced a successful YouTube series called "Ringbrothers University." As time passed, tech evolved and consumer tastes changed, and so did our tactics.

The brothers behind Ringbrothers are Mike and Jim Ring. Based in Spring Green, Wisconsin, the duo (and their very talented team) are like modern-day artists. They think of wild automotive visions that have never been created before and then execute them in carbon fiber and aluminum. Their car builds often cost close to seven figures, and their parts sell at a premium. But the brothers themselves are not digital natives. They don't spend much time online and don't really participate in social media personally. Authenticity is critical, so we work with them to do in-person appearances, podcast and TV interviews, and live chats on streaming platforms.

Their social channel—which is wildly popular and a huge traffic driver for the brand—is a balance of informative content and fun, irreverent memes, mostly thought up by our account lead, Eric, and executed by guys in the shop who like having fun on camera. The result is that the Rings get to be their true authentic selves, the brand continues to grow and reach new audiences, and the company benefits from a significant increase in recognition and revenue.

THE FUTURE OF PR AND THE ROLE OF AGENCIES

As we look to the future, the role of agencies will continue to evolve. The traditional boundaries between PR, marketing, creative, and branding are increasingly blurred, and the need for integrated strategies has never been greater. The digital landscape offers unprecedented opportunities for brands to engage directly with their audiences, but it also requires a strategic approach that leverages the right channels and messages at the right times.

The future of PR will be shaped by several key trends, including the rise of AI and automation, the increasing importance of authenticity and transparency, and the need for brands to be agile and responsive in a rapidly changing environment.

AI AND AUTOMATION: TOOLS, NOT REPLACEMENTS

AI and automation are transforming the PR landscape, offering new tools for data analysis, content creation, and audience engagement. However, these technologies are not replacements for human creativity and strategy. They are tools that can enhance our capabilities, allowing us to work more efficiently and effectively.

For example, AI can help us analyze vast amounts of data to identify trends and insights that inform our strategies. It can automate routine tasks, freeing up time for more strategic activities. But the creative process—the ability to craft compelling narratives, build relationships, and engage audiences on an emotional level—remains firmly in the realm of human expertise.

THE IMPORTANCE OF AUTHENTICITY AND TRANSPARENCY

In an age of information overload, authenticity and transparency are more important than ever. Consumers are increasingly savvy and can easily spot inauthentic or manipulative messaging. Brands that succeed in the future will be those that are honest, open, and genuine in their communications.

The Pepsi commercial featuring Kendall Jenner is a prime example of what not to do. The ad was widely criticized for its inauthentic and insensitive portrayal of social justice issues. In contrast, the Stanley response to the viral TikTok video was authentic and heartfelt, resonating with audiences and driving significant brand growth.

AGILITY AND RESPONSIVENESS IN A RAPIDLY CHANGING ENVIRONMENT

The PR landscape is constantly evolving, and brands need to be agile and responsive to stay ahead. This requires a deep understanding of the current environment, a willingness to experiment with new approaches, and the ability to pivot quickly when necessary.

The COVID-19 pandemic highlighted the importance of agility and responsiveness. Brands that were able to adapt quickly to the new reality, leveraging digital channels and virtual events to engage with their audiences, were able to maintain their relevance and continue driving growth.

BUILDING AND MAINTAINING RELATIONSHIPS

At the heart of effective PR is the ability to build and maintain relationships. This is true whether we're talking about media relations, influencer partnerships, or direct engagement with consumers. Relationships are built on trust, and trust is earned through consistent, authentic communication.

One of our key strengths at Kahn Media is our ability to leverage existing media relationships and forge new ones with complementary brands, influencers, and specialist media reps. This ability to connect and collaborate with the right people is crucial in today's media landscape.

CONCLUSION: THE ROAD AHEAD

The journey that allowed me to write this book started almost thirty years ago, when I was still in high school and had the crazy idea to take some pictures of my car parked on the grass at a local park and then write an article about it, which I sent to some of the biggest car magazines in the world. A few of them bit, and I landed the car on the cover of not one but *three* major magazines the same year. I was doing PR at sixteen and didn't even know what that was. Five years later I was working for the very company that I sent those letters to, a few years after that I was working as an editor at one of the first major blogs devoted to car news and reviews, and less than a decade later I was at the helm of a major marketing and PR firm working for some of the best brands in the world.

It has been a wild ride, and my motto throughout my entire career has been "make every mistake once." I don't have all the answers, and as both business and technology continue to evolve and change the way we connect brands with consumers, there is only one way I've been able to constantly stay ahead of the curve and keep my own company and the brands that hire us successful and focused on the future—we constantly try new tactics, study the results, learn from our mistakes, and repeat the stuff that worked, until it doesn't. Then we start again.

I wish there was a one-size-fits-all instruction manual for achieving success in PR and marketing in the current environment. But with so many platforms, creators, variations in the earned/owned/paid media ecosystem, and an environment that is affected as much by changing algorithms and consumer tastes as it is by the economy and other traditional business ecosystem indicators, nothing printed on paper will be relevant in a few months or years. Instead, I hope this book helps you build a mindset and a framework for achieving PR and marketing success today and into the future. That's why I avoided "to build more sales, do X, Y and Z" type instruction and instead tried to contextualize the current environment and offer insight into how people, brands, and companies large and small can operate (and succeed!) in a world where budgets and business size are less relevant than ever. All it takes is strategic planning, creativity, and a lot of effort.

As we conclude this journey through the evolving landscape of PR and marketing, it's clear that the road ahead is both challenging and exciting. The principles of effective PR—authenticity, transparency, storytelling, and relationship building—remain as relevant as ever, even as the tools and channels we use continue to evolve.

Working with a PR agency can provide the expertise, resources, and strategic insight needed to navigate this complex environment. Whether it's leveraging new technologies, crafting compelling narratives, or building meaningful relationships, a good agency can help you achieve your business goals and drive long-term success.

The power of PR can take your business to the next level by helping you to authentically engage with key audiences more quickly and impactfully than ever before. Are you ready to hit the road?

We've reached the end of our journey, but your journey is just beginning. I encourage you to take advantage of the self-diagnostic and PR planning app in the appendix. Just use the QR code to start the evaluation to discover the next steps for your PR journey.

PR/MARKETING CHECKLIST

→ Kick things off with clear goals. Start by asking yourself, "What do I want to achieve with my PR and marketing efforts?" Be specific. Break down your goals by product, service, target audience, or even geography.

→ Get your brand message straight. What's your brand all about? What do you want to achieve in each area of focus?

→ Know your audience. Who are you targeting? Who's going to be interested in what you're offering? The more you understand your target audience, the better you can tailor your strategy to them.

→ Build your audience profiles or persona(s). Based on your understanding of your target audience, create detailed personas or profiles. This will help keep your focus consistent and relevant. Use research, surveys, or interviews to make these as relevant as possible.

➔ Clarify your strategy. Now it's time to put together a comprehensive PR and marketing strategy. Consider your objectives, goals, target audience, and available resources. Your strategy will guide everything you do.

➔ Find the best balance of your media mix. Are you making the most of earned, owned, and paid media? Each has its own strengths, and they can work together to maximize your reach and engagement.

➔ Create on-brand content. Your content should be a natural extension of your brand's message and should resonate with your target audience. It should also support your overall brand narrative. This could range from paid advertising to social media to events, videos, webinars, and more.

➔ Connect with your key audiences directly. Identify ways to interact directly with customers, potential customers, and media enthusiasts. Are you engaging with them effectively?

➔ Maximize your media relationships. Are you using your existing media connections? Are you actively seeking new relationships with brands, influencers, and specialist media that complement your brand?

➔ Implement integrated marketing strategies. Consider how tactics like newsjacking, social media content, video news releases (VNRs), and other communication strategies could reinforce your messaging.

➔ Blend old and new media. Make sure you're using both traditional and modern media outlets to reach your audience.

➔ Launch your campaign. This could involve getting your brand and products featured in leading mainstream and vertical/enthusiast digital, print, and broadcast outlets, as well as with top social media influencers and content creators.

➔ Track your progress. Are you using the right tools to measure the success of your PR and marketing strategy? Use tools like Google Analytics, Semrush,

Qualtrics, HubSpot, Salesforce, and others to track key performance indicators (KPIs) and evaluate campaign effectiveness.

➔ Monitor audience responses and manage relationships. Keep an eye on how your audience is responding to your strategy. Are you managing any potential issues that may arise from direct interactions with consumers? Are you prepared to deal with any reputational risks or crises that may arise?

➔ Follow up and measure success. Keep track of your campaign's success and adjust as necessary to ensure that you're continually on track to achieve your goals.

CONTACT

I LOOK FORWARD TO CONTINUING THE JOURNEY!

You can reach me via email at **dan@kahnmedia.com,**
and connect with me on LinkedIn at
https://www.linkedin.com/in/kahnmedia.

To see how we're navigating the rapidly changing marketing landscape
scan the QR code below or visit us at **www.kahnmedia.com.**

www.ingramcontent.com/pod-product-compliance
Lightning Source LLC
Chambersburg PA
CBHW031504180326
41458CB00044B/6687/J